Mount Washington

A Guide and Short History

Mount

Washington

A Guide and Short History

by Peter Randall

Foreword by Sherman Adams

University Press of New England

Hanover, New Hampshire 1974

The University Press
of New England

Sponsoring Institutions

Brandeis University

Clark University

Dartmouth College

University of New Hampshire

The University of Rhode Island

University of Vermont

Library of Congress Catalog Card Number: 73–85237

ISBN Clothbound: 0–87451–088–0

ISBN Paperbound: 0–87451–089–9

Printed in the United States of America

For Judy, Deidre, Davis,

and Katelyn, who love

the mountains as much

as I do

Foreword

For a fortunate few, the subject of this little guide and history has provided the most exciting experience of their lives. Speaking for myself, the first ascent in the dead of winter up the headwall of Tuckerman's Ravine, then over the cone of Mt. Washington, buffeted by zero degree gales, in thick clouds and driving snow that sealed the eyelids frozen shut in a blink, hunting for rime-covered cairns to the summit, was a memorable but hardly congenial introduction to this mountain.

With many more desirable ways to climb Mt. Washington, the visitor can come to know the highest peak in the northeast United States in reasonable safety. Even though there is less than an even chance of an unlimited view from the summit, the experience is worth it, no matter what the conditions. In a thick cloud cover, with sight limited to a few feet, there comes a feeling of ultimate loneliness, a dissociation from reality. Wandering away from landmarks a short distance brings a sense of isolation and the helpless horror which possesses one who becomes lost or benighted on this cold and forbidding New England mountain. To understand these sensations can be a new and strange experience.

Besides weather, Mt. Washington is many other things. It is masses of rock and great glacial cirques. Part of it is alpine flowers and plants, lichens and puckerbrush. It is the cog railway and the carriage road and myriad trails and guide boards, all to make it accessible for some thirteen weeks in the summer and early fall to experience and enjoy.

The old buildings at the summit, needing relocation and replacement, are reminiscent of others, burned or demolished, which stood here in earlier years to provide refuge and shelter, bed and board, and even printed news of the goings on in the White Mountains.

To love and to understand Mt. Washington is to know the significant events of its history, the remarkable exploits of Ethan Allen Crawford, the guide and innkeeper; the work and discoveries of Dr. Edward Tuckerman, the lichenologist; the research and collections of William Oakes, the botanist, and others of the pioneer scientists, meterologists, and geologists who were drawn to this mountain for its sources of knowledge in each of their particular fields.

A year or so before this book was written, the author asked my opinion whether a compendium of facts about Mt. Washington in the nature of a descriptive guide and history, together with some thoughts about protecting the surface of the mountain from human despoilage, would be a useful addition to the rather limited bibliography of the mountain. I thought it would. Whoever writes convincingly of Mt. Washington needs both accurate knowledge and an affinity for the rugged peak whose history reaches back to the origins of New Hampshire and the tourist, the summer boarder and the city folks who once populated the miles of hotel verandas in the White Mountains every year from late June through Labor Day.

This guide and history has been carefully researched and written. More facts are collected about the mountain, as well as accounts of historic events that happened here, than have appeared before in a book of this kind. It serves a useful purpose to those who are about to ascend the mountain, to those who already have and want to know more about what they have seen, and to still others who never saw or intend to see the mountain but want to know something about it.

Allusions to the future use and occupancy of Mt. Washington bring attention to the need for decent and adequate structures and facilities to accommodate properly the people who visit here from other states and who go back home feeling critical of the conditions presently encountered on the mountain.

As I write, the third successive State Commission has completed and submitted recommendations, this time for a rehabilitation of the summit, and a plan for its operation as the loftiest and most recent addition to the state park system. Those who ask that the present summit building be preserved should know that it is obsolete and rotten, and has been kept in presentable condition only by facial treatment that conceals its current condition. The structure proposed by the present Commission, of wood, stone, and glass, will blend unobtrusively into the northern slope of the summit and is designed to provide permanent quarters for the observatory and its exhibits, space for search and rescue equipment, a refuge, and public conveniences, all of which look well ahead to future demands upon the park.

More pride in the facilities at the summit will mean better care taken of the whole mountain. The wider the interest taken in the protection of Mt. Washington the better the prospects will be for the reconstruction of the summit structures presently so sorely needed. This volume will surely contribute to the public awareness of the mountain and add measurably to the interest taken in its preservation.

Lincoln, N.H.   Sherman Adams
August 1973

Preface

Mt. Washington's rugged beauty, its harsh weather conditions, and its proximity to population centers have combined to make it one of the world's most fascinating mountains. With an elevation of 6288 feet, it is the highest mountain in the Northeast, and when combined with the rest of the Presidential Range of which it is a part, the seven-square-mile alpine zone is far more spectacular and interesting than the slightly higher tree-covered peaks in the Great Smokies of North Carolina.

Although Mt. Washington is considered only a minor peak when compared to many famous mountains in other parts of the world, it is nevertheless high enough so that the upper portion of the mountain projects into a major storm track, producing on the summit the most severe weather conditions known outside polar regions. Because of the harsh climate, the unique plant life of the mountain's alpine zone is closely related to that of Labrador, some 600 miles north. For nearly two centuries scientists have journeyed here to study geology, botany, and weather.

While explorers were still seeking out the best routes through the Rockies, hundreds of tourists were walking and riding on horseback to the summit of Mt. Washington. No other mountain can boast of having, in its history, a carriage road, railway, daily newspaper, four different hotels, two weather observatories, a radio station, and a television station, in addition to miles of hiking trails.

None of this would have been possible if Mt. Washington were situated in a remote area. For more than 150 years, summer travelers have journeyed to the White Mountains and Mt. Washington in particular, to escape from their hot, congested cities. First on horseback, then by stagecoach and railroad, and now by automobile, tourists have been able to reach these mountains with relative ease. Innkeepers and other entrepreneurs were quick to see the potential profits to be gained from catering to travelers. By the 1870's the White Mountains were host to thousands of visitors, and a trip to the summit of Mt. Washington was for increasing numbers an essential part of a summer vacation in northern New England.

It is estimated that today the summit is visited annually by some 50,000 hikers, the same number of Cog Railway passengers, and 115,000 Carriage Road travelers. With some 60 million people within a day's ride of the mountain, it can be expected that the total will continue to increase.

In preparing this guide and short history, we are carrying on a White Mountain guidebook tradition that began in the 1830's and continued through the early years of this century. It is our hope that those who read this book will come to share our affection for Mt. Washington and our concerns for its future. Although its core may be solid rock, the surface of the mountain is fragile, and only by wise use and continuing awareness of the destructibility of the plants, lichens, and struggling forests will future generations be able to get the same enjoyment from Mt. Washington that we all share today.

This book could not have been produced without the assistance of Douglas Philbrook, manager of the Mt. Washington Carriage Road. His great knowledge of the White Mountains and willingness to share the contents of his excellent collection of material on the area have made possible the transformation of an idea into reality. For his time, patience, counsel, and ready wit, I am in his debt.

The interest and support of former New Hampshire Governor Sherman Adams is also appreciated. For his careful reading of the manuscript and for writing the foreword, I am grateful.

Among many others who have assisted, I wish to thank C. Francis Belcher, Executive Director, Appalachian Mountain Club; Paul C. Dunn, General Manager and Robert L. Kent, Trainmaster, Mt. Washington Railway Company; Guy Gosselin, Chief Observer, Mt. Washington Observatory; Dr. Richard P. Goldthwait, Department of Geology, Ohio State University; Dr. Donald H. Chapman, Department of Geology, University of New Hampshire; Dr. Frederic L. Steele, teacher of science, the White Mountain School, Littleton; Winston Pote, photographer, Lancaster; Lee Vincent of WMTW-TV and WMTQ-FM, Gorham; Walter Wright, Curator of Rare Books and Chief of Special Collections, Baker Library, Dartmouth College; George Kent, Stinson House, Rumney; James Bolquerin, Rockport, Massachusetts; David Horne, Director, University Press of New England; Mary H. Arnett, Portsmouth, who turned my rough typing into a readable manuscript; and my wife, Judy, for her patience and willingness to share my affections with a mountain.

Hampton, N.H.   P.R.
August 1973

Contents

List of Illustrations

1 Introduction

The White Mountains were 260 million years old when the Rocky Mountains were being formed, but their recorded history does not begin until 1524, when Giovanni da Verrazano reported seeing the Presidential Range while sailing off what is now Portsmouth, New Hampshire. Other sea captains made later observations. The name "Christall Hills" appears in a 1628 narrative, and John Josselyn's *New England's Rarities Discovered,* 1672, uses for the first time the name "White Mountains." They are labeled "White Hills" on John Foster's 1677 map of New England.

The first recorded ascent of Mt. Washington was in May or June of 1642, when Darby Field of Exeter, New Hampshire, reached the top with two Indian companions. Presumably he followed the Ellis River north from where it joins the Saco and then climbed Boott Spur to the summit. The adventure aroused so much interest that Field returned with five or six friends a month later. In August of the same year,

North

17°

Legend:
◇ Alpine Garden
+ Lion Head
▢ Hermit Lake
▲ Appalachian Trail
▲ Mountain Summit

Carter Range (N, Middle, S)

Carter Dome

Crystal Cascade
Sherburne Ski Trail

Glen House site

Wildcat Mountain

Wildcat Range (lesser summits)

Pinkham Notch

Old Jackson Road
Pinkham Notch camp

P/O

Glen Boulder Trail

Peabody River

Peabody River West Branch

Dolly Copp Campground
Great Gulf Trail

Osgood Trail

Mt. Madison
Madison Gulf Trail

Mt. Sam Adams Trail

Mt. Adams

Mt. Jefferson

Carriage Road

Crag Trail

Nelson Crag Trail

Huntington Ravine

Mt. Washington Path

Tuckerman Ravine

Boott Spur Trail

Boott Spur

Mt. Isolation

Great Gulf Trail

Gulfside Trail

Spaulding Lake

Mt. Clay

Israel Ridge Path

Oakes Gulf

Westside Trail
Burt Ravine
Ammonoosuc Ravine
Ammonoosuc Ravine Trail

Ammonoosuc Cog Railway
River

Base Station/Marshfield
Lakes of the Clouds hut
Mt. Monroe

Mt. Franklin

Mt. Eisenhower

Edmands Path

Mt. Clinton

Webster Cliff Trail

Mt. Jackson

Mt. Clinton Road

Crawford Path

Crawford House

Mt. Mitten ▲

Mt. Dartmouth ▲

Road to Base Station

Bridle Path

Fabyans

Mt. Washington Hotel
Bretton Woods

Route 302

Mt. Tom ▲

C

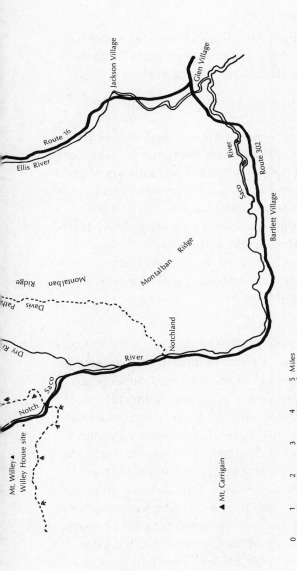

1. Map of the area.

Thomas Gorges and Richard Vines also reached the summit, but from that time until the 1770's only a few others dared to challenge this rocky, wind-swept peak.

It is likely that Field's party was the first to reach the summit, for to the Indians the mountain was sacred. They called it Agiocochook or Waumbeket Methna, meaning Mountain of the Snowy Forehead or Home of the Great Spirit, and would not climb it be-cause it was the home of their gods and they feared to intrude. Perhaps the storms that swirl about the summit in all seasons of the year had much to do with both their veneration and their reluctance to attempt the climb.

Like the Indians, the first settlers in the North Coun-try avoided the mountains, preferring the farming land in the broad valleys along the Connecticut River, a region known as Upper Coos, for which the northernmost county of New Hampshire was later named. In 1770 or 1771, however, Timothy Nash, a hunter in search of a moose, climbed a tree on Cherry Mountain (near the town of Jefferson) and far to the south saw a huge defile or "notch." He passed through it, following the Saco River south-ward, and went on to Portsmouth to tell Governor John Wentworth of his discovery. Realizing the economic and political importance of a shorter route between the seacoast and the settlements in the Upper Coos, Wentworth promised to grant a large tract of land to Nash if he could bring a horse through the notch alive and on to Portsmouth. Nash, assisted by Benjamin Sawyer, apparently accomplished the feat, since the grant of land was made and became known as Nash and Sawyer Location. Within a few years a rough road had been cut through this mountain pass (later named Crawford Notch after its first settler), at one stretch crossing the Saco River thirty-two times in twenty miles. Thus began one of the most important eras in the mountains.

The first settler in this great western valley of Mt. Washington was Abel Crawford, who built a rough cabin in 1791 near the area of Fabyans on present-day Route 302. A year later he sold it to his father-in-law, Eleazer Rosebrook, and with his family moved twelve miles south near the present Notchland railroad crossing in Hart's Location.

A Notch Turnpike was incorporated in 1803, the same year that Rosebrook, who had already been hosting farmers en route to and from the markets in Portland and Portsmouth, built near his cabin a two-story house with accommodations for travelers, the first hotel in the White Mountains. He remained here until his death in 1817.

It was Ethan Allen Crawford, Abel's son, however, who was to achieve the greatest fame among those early settlers. Nearly six feet, three inches tall and of great strength, Ethan grew up in Crawford Notch, helping his father work the land and learning to hunt the abundant wild animals. In 1811 he left home to enlist in the army, intending to settle away from the mountains, but in 1816 he returned at the request of his ailing grandfather Rosebrook. He inherited the property and its debts a year later, when the old man died. Ethan and his first cousin, Lucy Howe, who had helped nurse old Rosebrook, were married in that same year. Her *History of the White Mountains,* published in 1846, is the first printed history of this region.

In 1819 Ethan, with the help of his father, built the first trail to the summit of Mt. Washington. Named the Crawford Path, it began opposite the present Crawford House on Route 302 and is the oldest continuously used mountain trail in America. It still follows Ethan's old route most of the way. His brother Thomas improved the trail as a bridle path in 1840, and Abel, then 75, was the first to ride a horse to the top.

Ethan improved his house, which had been built as an inn, but he lost the fruits of his labor when it burned in 1818. The smaller dwelling that immediately took its place was able to accommodate only a half dozen or so overnight guests. It was not until 1825 that he was able to enlarge the structure and operate once again a fair-sized hostelry. But travelers could stay at Abel's Crawford House, built prior to 1820 at Notchland, and in 1829 Ethan and his father built still another inn at the Gateway to the Notch, not far from the present Crawford House. Managed from that time until 1852 by Thomas Crawford, it, too, was destroyed by fire, in 1854. (See also below, pages 8–9.)

In addition to being an unequaled guide, Ethan literally carried men and women over portions of his trails, and it was he who showed the way to the early botanists who flocked to the mountains. In addition to the Crawford Path, he built in 1821 a bridle path to the present Cog Railway Base Station and a foot trail from there to the summit. That trail was improved as a bridle path by Horace Fabyan about 1840. Ethan carried huge loads to the top, acting, he said, as a pack mule when New Hampshire Secretary of State Philip Carrigain and his party climbed the range in 1820 to name most of the peaks of the Presidentials: Madison, Adams, Jefferson, Monroe, Franklin, and Pleasant (now Eisenhower).

In 1821 Ethan guided three young ladies to the summit—the Misses Austin of Portsmouth. They were the first women to reach the top. The first to climb in winter were two of Ethan's daughters, in 1874.

The first buildings on the mountain were three small stone huts constructed by Ethan in 1823 near the site of the present Gulf tank on the Cog Railway. Because of interior dampness, the huts were little used. The following year Ethan brought a large tent and a sheet metal stove from Portsmouth and carried them to the top. The elements made short work of the tent.

Only a vigorously healthy man could have withstood the rigor of life in the Notch. In 1837, worn out from his labors and debts, Ethan left the Notch for Guildhall, Vermont, where he had been born, and the landlordship of his inn passed to Horace Fabyan, for whom the later hotel and railroad junction were named. Ethan returned in 1843 to rent the White Mountain House, an inn only a mile away from his former home. Here he died three years later, at the age of 54. Although he was not to reap the profits that accrued to later hotelmen of the region, he will always be remembered as the man who did the most to introduce the public to the White Mountains.

The tradition of innkeeping established by the Rosebrook and Crawford families was continued in the years after Ethan's death. The large hotels later to be built in the region of Crawford Notch were the first Crawford House, 1852-53; the present Crawford House, 1859; Twin Mountain House, 1869-

70; Fabyan House, 1873; Mount Pleasant House, 1876; and the present Mount Washington Hotel at Bretton Woods, 1902. The Golden Era of White Mountain hotels was under way, and almost every community in the region eventually had one or several of these 50 to 250-room hostelries. There were, in fact, more overnight accommodations in this area in 1900 than at present. Many of the old hotels have been destroyed by fire, and although motels have been built as replacements, they are rarely as large as the structures existing earlier. Of the hotels of that era in the immediate vicinity of Mt. Washington, only the Crawford House and the Mount Washington Hotel remain. The Fabyan House burned in 1951, and the Mount Pleasant House was torn down during the Depression.

Because Crawford Notch, on the west slope, offered the best route between the coastal markets and settlements of the North Country, it was developed earlier and more extensively than was the eastern, or Pinkham, notch. The latter remained uninhabited until 1827, when young Hayes Copp built a small cabin at the site of the present Dolly Copp Campground on Route 16. Hayes married Dolly Emery in 1831 after toiling alone for four years to carve out a farm in the wilderness. When Daniel Pinkham, for whom the notch is named, cut a road from Jackson to Randolph between 1824 and 1834, it passed the Copp homestead, and for the next forty years the

2. *Mt. Washington from the Conway Road. From an illustration by Harry Fenn in* Picturesque America, *1872.*

Copps took in travelers while greatly expanding the size of their farm.

A few other families settled in this region, but the first major developments did not come until 1851, when the Atlantic and St. Lawrence Railroad, the first to enter the White Mountains, began passenger service to Gorham, where the Alpine House opened. In the same year the first Glen House was built, and in spite of the competition from a number of other hotels which later dotted the western side of the mountain, it became one of the largest and most popular of all the resorts. On their Golden Wedding Anniversary, the Copps separated, Dolly saying that fifty years was long enough to live with any man. Their farm and holdings were equally divided; Dolly went to live with a daughter in Auburn, Maine, and Hayes went back to his native Stow in Maine.

Following the construction of The Glen House, the next important event in Pinkham Notch was the completion of the Carriage Road in 1861. Its story is told in the following chapter. Of later importance too were the opening of the Appalachian Mountain Club's Pinkham Notch camp in 1921 and the development of the Wildcat Mountain Recreation and Ski Area in 1958 (see also pages 139, 142).

Before the growth of tourism, interest in the mountains had been shown by scientists. In 1784 the first purely scientific expedition came to the mountain, led by the Reverend Dr. Jeremy Belknap of Dover, author of the state's first history, and the Reverend Manasseh Cutler of Ipswich, Massachusetts. Although Belknap was unable to reach the summit, others in the party did, becoming the first ever to spend a night on the top. They came seeking the same data that even today draw scientists in meteorology and botany. Dr. Cutler, for whom the stream flowing out of Tuckerman Ravine is named, was the first to describe in detail the mountain's unique alpine plants. Belknap and Cutler are credited with naming the mountain in honor of George Washington.

Dr. Cutler returned in 1804 for further botanical study, and he was followed in later years by, among others, Dr. Jacob Bigelow, Francis Boott, William Oakes, and Edward Tuckerman, all of whom added to the basic knowledge of the mountains and who have geographical features of the area bearing their names today. Oakes, whose visits occurred in the 1820's and 1840's, is remembered for his book *Scenery of the White Mountains,* first published in 1848 with intricate and excellent lithographs. It remains one of the best and most beautiful books ever to appear about these mountains.

The first detailed geographical report on the mountains was published in 1844 by Charles T. Jackson, State Geologist, but a more comprehensive study was produced in 1877 as Volume Two of C. H. Hitchcock's *Geology of New Hampshire*. (For additional reading sources, see below, page 149). Hitchcock began his work in 1868 and with the aid of many others conducted surveys throughout the mountains. Part of his project included the first winter occupation of the summit, in 1871–72 (below, page 76).

The growth of tourism and the unique scientific value of the entire mountain region both led to increased concern about the future of this area. Between 1890 and 1910, logging companies and disastrous fires laid waste vast areas of forest. Despite years of opposition (not all of it by the logging companies, who were sometimes glad to unload cut-over land), the White Mountain National Forest was created in 1911 after the Weeks Act granted authority to acquire private land. A tract of 85,592 acres, including Mt. Washington, was added to this forest in 1914. In 1973 the White Mountain National Forest comprised 728,516 acres, of which 45,944 were in Maine.

2 The Carriage Road

When the Carriage Road officially opened on August 8, 1861, the occasion marked the completion of an amazing engineering feat that had been dreamed about for years, perhaps from those early days when the first footpath was built in 1819.

Although many talked about the project, it remained for General David C. Macomber of Middletown, Connecticut, to provide the imagination and determination necessary to make the eight-mile road a reality. Through his efforts a charter was acquired from the State of New Hampshire in 1853, and in August of that year the first meeting of the Mount Washington Road Company was held in the Alpine House at Gorham. With Macomber as president, the Company was organized and authorized to issue $50,000 worth of stock. A year later a surveying party went to work.

A rugged bridle path, known to have existed as early as 1852, rose about six steep miles from The Glen to the summit, and it provided the route for part of the road. The survey party eventually laid out a more gradual route, following the most picturesque line feasible; it rose some 4600 feet in eight miles, with an average grade of only 12 percent. Work began in 1854, the same year as the survey, with the first contract set at $8000 per mile, a huge sum in those days. Using the most primitive of methods—hand labor, horses, oxen, and black powder for blasting—the crew completed two miles by 1855 and two years later reached the halfway point near the Horn: Here work was halted for two years, the original company failed financially, and a discouraged General Macomber left the mountains, never to return.

In June 1859 the present Mount Washington Summit Road Company was incorporated, and with $100,000 in capital stock as backing, work began anew. Construction on the upper mountain moved quickly, and by July 1861 Joseph M. "Landlord" Thompson, proprietor of The Glen House, drove the first horse and wagon to the top. He required the assistance of men in the party to help keep the wagon upright over the last few hundred feet, which had not yet been completed. But he made it.

Finally, on August 8, about 200 people gathered on the summit for the gala occasion celebrating the grand opening. George W. Lane arrived driving a

Concord Coach, pulled by eight horses and loaded with passengers. The event heralded a new era of prosperity for this part of the White Mountains. With the opening of the Road, tourists could journey by train to Gorham and then change to coaches for the drive to The Glen House, where they boarded twelve-passenger wagons for the summit.

The novelty of the Road helped make The Glen House the most popular resort in the mountains. It was subsequently expanded several times, and by the 1870's it could house 500 guests, who paid $4.50 per day for board, room, transportation to the daily trains at Gorham, and the privilege of relaxing on the 700-foot long piazzas, enjoying one of the most spectacular panoramic views in the mountains.

The original Glen House burned in 1884, and another built in 1885 met the same fate eight years later. A third, together with sheds and barns, burned in 1924. The fourth, much smaller than the first two, was destroyed by fire in 1967.

When this, the world's first mountain toll road, opened, tolls were charged by the mile for the entire round trip of 16 miles. Those on foot paid two cents a mile; those on horseback, three cents; and each person in a carriage, five cents. Rates from four to eight cents per mile were charged for various combinations of wagons and teams. By 1864 The

3. View of the Carriage Road along Five Mile Grade. The region known as the Horn is in the center of the photograph, with the Half-Way House at the lower right. Photo by Dick Smith, courtesy of the Mt. Washington Summit Road Company.

Glen House wagons alone were carrying between thirty and fifty passengers per day. When the Cog Railway opened in 1869, many people were eager to spend a day going up one way and down the other, returning to their base via stage coach through the notches.

The first mountain wagons on the Carriage Road were made especially for that purpose by the Abbot-Downing Company of Concord, builders of the picturesque stagecoaches seen in western movies. When the Carriage Road company began using auto "stages" in 1912, the first of the new gasoline-powered vehicles was a Thomas Flyer, followed by a Knox, a Peerless, and a Chandler. Soon afterward Packards were introduced, then Pierce Arrows until 1938. The public was allowed to drive motor vehicles on the Road beginning in 1908; each car with two passengers was charged $3.00. Since 1911 the toll for each car and driver has been set at $5.00, the price currently in effect (see below, page 25).

Today the Road is one of the most popular attractions in the White Mountains. Its smoothly graded surface, partially paved, is traveled safely by hundreds of people daily from May through October, either in their own cars or in the Company's modern stages. The Road's excellent condition and safety record bear testimony to the capable engineering of its builders and the good maintenance program of the Company today. In fact, the only passenger fatality related to the Road throughout its long history occurred in 1880 when a drunken mountain wagon driver lost control of his team below the Half-Way House. One woman was killed and several people were injured when the wagon overturned.

In addition to its use by tourists, the Carriage Road serves as a year-round supply route for the people who man the various summit facilities. Throughout the winter, supplies, equipment, and crew members are regularly hauled up the road in large snow vehicles. The Army and Navy have also used the road as a supply route when conducting various research projects on the mountain (see below, page 84).

The desire to set records or to do something for the first time has been keen in the Mt. Washington area, and completion of the Carriage Road opened up a whole new area of challenge, both serious and humorous. Since the 1850's there has been no lack of competitors:

July 25, 1855: A 230-pound woman won a $1000 wager by walking to the summit and back in one day, then danced at The Glen House all evening.

August 2, 1857: Using the half completed road as far as it went, George S. Dana counted 16,925 steps from The Glen House to the summit.

December 7, 1858: First winter ascent of Mt. Washington, by Deputy Sheriff Lucius Hartshorn and Benjamin F. Osgood, who subsequently became a well-known mountain guide and trail builder. They made the trip to place an attachment on the summit buildings, and returned the same day.

February 10, 1862: First overnight winter journey to the summit, by John N. Spaulding, Chapin C. Brooks, and Franklin White. Because of a storm they were forced to stay in the Summit House for two days and nights.

1875: Harlan P. Amen, principal of Phillips Exeter Academy, ran up in one hour and 57 minutes and ran down in 54 minutes.

August 22, 1882: James W. Brown, with a six-horse mountain wagon, drove dignitaries to the summit in two hours and 3 minutes.

August 11, 1883: C. E. Heath made a descent on a Victor tricycle in 55 minutes.

September 6, 1887: The record for a horse-drawn ascent was set by Charles O'Hara—one hour, 9 minutes, 27 seconds.

August 31, 1899: Mr. and Mrs. Freelan O. Stanley were the first to drive an engine-powered vehicle, a steam Locomobile, to the top. Running time: two hours and 10 minutes.

August 25, 1903: First officially timed ascent by automobile (one hour, 48 minutes), by L. J. Phelps in a car of his own make.

1904: First National Hill Climbing Competition, Francis E. Stanley with a seven-horsepower steamer, 28 minutes, 19 2/5 seconds; and Harry Harkness with a 60-horsepower gasoline Mercedes, 24 minutes, 37 3/5 seconds.

August 16, 1904: George S. Foster ran to the summit in one hour, 42 minutes.

In 1905 the White Mountain region was the scene of the first Glidden Tour, which included another assault on Mt. Washington and a new motor vehicle record. Bill Hilliard drove his Napier to the summit in 20 minutes, 58 2/5 seconds.

February 1907: Norman Libby and a companion made the first road ascent via skis. They went to the Half-Way House. The return trip was made in 20 minutes—which was remarkable considering the type of equipment then available.

1913: First round trip to the summit on skis, by Carl E. Shumway, Fred H. Harris, and Joseph Y.

Cheney, all members of the Dartmouth Outing Club, formed by Harris in 1910.

March 30, 1926: Famed musher Arthur T. Walden, with friends and photographers along to help, drove the first team of huskies to the summit and back in 15 hours.

April 3, 1932: Mrs. Florence Clark became the first to drive a sled dog team to the summit unassisted.

Over the years both automobile and foot races have been held on the road, and records have been constantly broken. On July 9, 1961, the day of the last auto race, Bill Rutan set the existing record of nine minutes, 13 seconds, driving a car he had built from Volkswagen and Porsche parts. This is nearly one mile a minute over the eight-mile course with 99 curves, some of them fewer than 50 yards apart.

Fred Norris set the foot-race record on July 15, 1962, with a time of one hour, 4 minutes, 57 seconds. The Run to the Clouds is sponsored annually by the Mount Washington Summit Road Company, usually in June, with over 100 entrants.

In 1972 the record for the fastest bicycle trip to the summit was set by Jim Farnsworth in one hour, 40 minutes.

THE ASCENT

The spectacular ride to the summit via the Carriage Road begins at the toll station on the west side of Route 16 in Pinkham Notch. Known as The Glen, this area has been popular since 1851, when the first Glen House was built.

Visitors using the toll road may drive up in their own vehicles or may ride in the modern "stages" operated by the Glen and Mount Washington Stage Company. Throughout most of the summer, the road is open for private cars to make the ascent from 7:00 a.m. to 8:00 p.m., with shorter hours early and late in the season. Tolls for the round trip are as follows: Car and driver—$5.00; Motorcycle and driver—$3.00; Each adult passenger—$1.00; children 5 to 11—50¢; Children under 5—free. One-way tolls are slightly less. These rates have remained unchanged since 1911.

Stage service via chauffered Company vehicle, for those who do not want to drive up in their own cars, is available at the base from 8:00 a.m. to 4:30 p.m. Round-trip stage fares are as follows: Adults—$5.00; Children 5 to 11—$2.50; Children under 5 —free. There is no charge for hikers or bicyclists. Buses, mobile homes, and the larger pickup campers are not allowed. In winter all vehicles are banned from the Road except for the snow machines

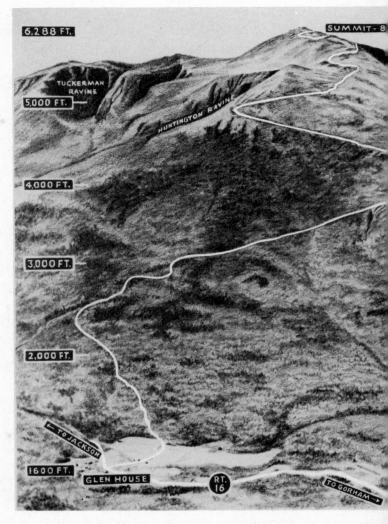

4. *Artist's sketch of Carriage Road route to the summit. Courtesy of the Mt. Washington Summit Road Company.*

that haul supplies to the summit facilities. Depending on weather conditions, the road is open from mid-May until late October.

The eight-mile, smoothly graded road ascends dramatically over the vast flanks and spurs of Mt. Washington, giving the rider or hiker a vivid sense of the massive size of the highest mountain in the Northeast. The first four miles wind through thick woods. There are few open panoramic views, but the beauty of the forest, cut by many brooks flowing over roadside ledges, makes this portion of the trip a pleasant one.

Near the base, beech, various maples, and yellow and white birch predominate in the deciduous forest, accompanied by a mixture of white pine, balsam fir, and spruce; but as the altitude increases, confers gradually become prominent. Mountain ash first appears near the upper limits of tree growth.

Approximately two miles from the base and six miles from the summit, three hiking trails diverge left: the Old Jackson Road leads to the Appalachian Mountain Club's Pinkham Notch headquarters; the Raymond Path, to Tuckerman Ravine; and the Nelson Crag Trail, upward to the Cow Pasture at Mile 7. Just beyond the two-mile point the Madison Gulf Trail exits right across Great Gulf, terminating at the AMC's Madison Spring hut in the col (dip) between Mounts Madison and Adams.

Two and one half miles from the base (altitude 3000 feet), the trees begin to diminish in size, although this typically northern forest is still dense. The stunted growth becomes pronounced as the Half-Way House (3840 feet) is approached.

The oldest structure now on the mountain, the Half-Way House was built in 1855 as living quarters for the superintendent of the crews building the road. Later it housed the road's maintenance workers, and following World War II the Navy used the building as headquarters for a program to test cold-weather clothing and equipment. For a time in recent years one room was left open as a winter refuge, but now the building is completely closed.

The most striking change in the landscape occurs just above the four-mile marker, where the road turns sharply at the Horn (4000 feet). This is the timberline, and from here to about 5300 feet the predominant species, balsam fir and black spruce, form a krummholz forest—in which the trees grow as low, dense, twisted mats or shrubs. Even though a hundred years old, krummholz attains a height of only two or three feet. White birch and mountain ash also appear as krummholz at the lower elevation. Higher on the mountain, krummholz is scattered, growing adjacent to rocks in the lee of prevailing winds and mixed with a variety of alpine plants. Nearer the Horn, these trees cover large areas, making hiking off the trails extremely difficult. By forming krummholz as a defense against the harsh weather, especially the severe winds, trees are able to survive in this rugged terrain.

The view from the Horn is the first dramatic panorama seen from the Carriage Road. Great Gulf opens below, and beyond it, from the left, are Mt. Clay, seen over a shoulder of Washington, then Jefferson, Adams, Madison, and Pine. Beyond the latter opens the great Androscoggin River Valley, bordered on the north by the rugged Mahoosuc Range, which terminates in Grafton Notch. South of this large river is the Peabody River glen, across from which is the Carter-Moriah Range.

Just beyond the Horn, the Chandler Brook Trail exits right to connect with the Great Gulf Trail, and four and one half miles from the base the Winter Cutoff road diverges right. It is used by the large snow vehicles to avoid drifts, which accumulate to great depths along the Five Mile Grade and Cragway (see below).

Three miles from the summit, the view at Mile 5 (4650 feet) overlooks the Androscoggin and Peabody River valleys to the north. Again the Mahoosuc

Range is seen, and beyond it rises Sunday River Whitecap in Maine. The near range to the east, running south from the Androscoggin, begins with Moriah and includes the Imp, the Carters, and Carter Dome.

Ahead is a good turnout, five and one half miles from the base, offering the first high-altitude view of the summit. Southeast across Pinkham Notch a complex of ski trails and slopes can be seen on the northerly face of Wildcat Mountain. Beyond is the long ridge of Pleasant Mountain, and further to the southeast is Sebago Lake—both of them in Maine. Numerous other lakes come into view as the altitude increases. The Ellis River flows south out of Pinkham Notch to join the Saco River at Glen Village. Mt. Doublehead and a pyramidal Mt. Kearsarge North (both seen over the southern shoulder of Wildcat) can be observed rising out of this valley to the south. Near the turnout, the Nelson Crag Trail passes, and beyond can be seen the upper reaches of Huntington Ravine. Boott Spur, the southern wall of Tuckerman Ravine, forms the jagged lower horizon, with Mt. Washington's summit rising to the right, high above.

Beginning at 5½ miles from the base and located each half mile for the next two miles, are small winter emergency shelters built originally by the Air Force during a period of research work on the mountain and now maintained by the Mt. Washington Observatory. The tall poles occasionally seen are used by the road crews to locate the road and its culverts beneath deep snowdrifts when opening it in the spring.

Now the road reaches the grade called the Cragway, skirting under Nelson Crag and passing the upper end of the Winter Cutoff. Along the Cragway occur the greatest snowdrifts, approaching twenty-five feet in depth and presenting the most difficulty in opening the road each spring. Those driving the road early in the season are treated to a ride through these high drifts.

The Wamsutta Trail crosses just above the six-mile point (5300 feet and two miles from the summit). The upper limit of krummholz is on this section of the mountain, and vegetation, thick between the rocks and in broad grassy-appearing lawns, is mostly a combination of mosses, rush, heath, and sedges. Everywhere, the near landscape is composed of gray lichen-covered rocks and dark green vegetation.

Six and one half miles from the base (5500 feet) is Hairpin Turn, the sharpest cutback on the route; then the road lifts into the Cow Pasture one mile from the summit at Mile 7 (5900 feet). For at least one summer over a century ago, dairy cows were grazed here to provide a more convenient source of milk for guests at the Summit House and Tip Top House. The Nelson Crag Trail ends at the pasture's lower edge, and the Huntington Ravine Trail terminates at the upper limit, on the left. Here is the best place to park for a short walk along the trail south to the Alpine Garden (below, page 123). Although the trail is well marked, hikers should have a map, compass, windbreaker, sturdy shoes, and a friend along for the twenty-minute walk to the broad upland area.

The seven-mile point also offers the most dramatic view of the Northern Peaks, with every line of their U-shaped ravines and rugged summits clearly seen across Great Gulf.

Just ahead the road rims the upper reaches of Great Gulf. Here the slope drops away precipitously 1750 feet to tiny Spaulding Lake at the head of this huge glacier-scoured ravine. In 1959 the 5552-acre Great Gulf was designated as a wild area and was made a Wilderness Area in 1964. It is without roads or commercial activity of any sort, although it is cut by AMC trails, and the U.S. Forest Service maintains two shelters there for hikers. The Gulf is drained by the west branch of the Peabody River, considered good trout water. The area was named by Ethan Allen Crawford, who occasionally lost his way in bad weather and on one occasion reported that his party wandered to "the edge of a great gulf."

Now the road heads across Home Stretch Flat, one of the broad, flat grassy lawns below the summit, named by exhausted climbers knowing the summit to be only a few hundred feet higher. It parallels the tracks of the Cog Railway for a short distance, then swings east, where the traveler can look down on the Alpine Garden, Huntington Ravine (left), and the upper edges of Tuckerman Ravine (right). The road turns sharply and terminates at the Summit Road Company's large parking lots just below the summit buildings.

3 The Cog Railway

During a hike up the mountain in 1852, Sylvester Marsh, an inventor of sorts who had made a fortune in the Chicago meat-packing business, became lost in a storm and decided that there had to be an easier and safer way to reach the summit. A native of New Hampshire, Marsh appears to have adopted the idea for a cog system from Herrick Aiken and his son Walter, inventors from Franklin, New Hampshire. Their idea for a cog railway on the mountain had been turned down by leading railroad officials, but Marsh thought the idea had merit. By 1858 he had designed and built a small working model and, seeking the necessary charter, had brought it before the New Hampshire Legislature. Some said he might as well have asked for a charter to the moon, but his determination and his willingness to invest his own funds finally resulted in a charter for Mt. Washington and also for Mt. Lafayette, the highest peak in the Franconia Range.

Although many railroad men thought Marsh crazy,

he persisted. It was largely because of backing from other railroad visionaries, who saw the advantages of bringing passengers to the site, that $20,000 was raised for initial construction. The Mount Washington Steam Railway Company was formed in 1865, with Marsh as president and construction agent.

For $2000 the first engine was built during the following winter. Designed by Marsh, it was a crude affair, but it served as a test vehicle, was the workhorse engine during the railway's construction, and was used until it wore out about 1878.

The construction project was difficult enough, but logistics presented an equally severe problem. That first engine, with all supplies and equipment, had to be hauled by oxen from Littleton, twenty-five miles away. At what is now the Base Station but was then just wilderness, Marsh carved out a settlement to house and feed the crew. He built camps, horse barns, a saw mill—even a machine shop. A crude roadway to the Base Station followed the old bridle path cut in 1821 by Ethan Allen Crawford and later improved by Horace Fabyan. A more usable turnpike over this six-mile route was completed in 1869.

Because its upright boiler somewhat resembled a condiment cruet, the first engine was nicknamed "Peppersass." Following a successful public test

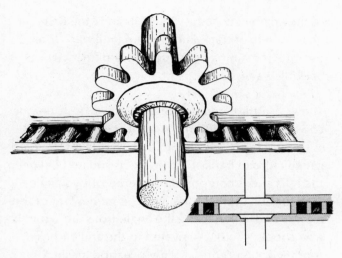

5. *Diagram of the cog mechanism*

of the engine on August 29, 1866, over the first quarter mile of track, the investing railroads took over the remaining construction, and financial backing was assured.

The key to the operation of the Railway is its unique cog or rack-and-pinion system. The engine pushes its car and is not coupled to it. Both ride on standard-gauge railroad tracks. The "rack" is situated between the rails and is composed of a series of two angle irons bolted firmly to the wooden framework of the railway bed. Connecting the angle irons are wrought-iron spools, 4" x 1½", riveted to the angle irons, four inches on center. Riding over and meshed between these spools run the two cog gears of the engine. The first engine had one pair of cylinders and only a single-drive cog wheel, rather than the double cogs now in use. On the cars there are cog gears and friction-band wheels for braking.

By 1867 the first half mile had been completed, and early in 1868 the Jacob's Ladder trestle (below, page 50) was finished. Actually, with the exception of the first quarter mile, the entire Railway is built as a trestle, ranging in height above the ground from two feet in some places to as much as thirty feet at Jacob's Ladder.

The first train reached the summit on July 3, 1869, marking the culmination of Sylvester Marsh's dream.

Although it is not known whether he got back his personal investment of $5000, it was certainly due to his determination that the project succeeded. He assumed little authority for the actual running of the railroad—that task fell to Walter Aiken—but for Marsh the completion was, no doubt, satisfaction enough.

Aiken, who ran the Railway until 1893, designed and built the second engine, the George Stephenson, and three others as well.

During the years after 1869 the growth of the tourist industry on the western side rivaled that centering in the Glen House complex on the east. Since the nearest hotel was some miles away, Marshfield House was built at the Base Station in 1871.

By 1875 the Boston, Concord, and Montreal Railroad from Littleton and the Portland and Ogdensburg Railroad from south of Crawford Notch met at Fabyans (see map, pages 2–3). The next year, the Boston, Concord, and Montreal built a spur from Fabyans to within a half mile of the Base Station.

The Cog Railway was subsequently extended down to connect with the new spur. In a matter of hours passengers could travel by rail from Boston to the summit of the mountain, where they could stay in the two-and-a-half-story Summit House built by

Walter Aiken in 1872–73. In 1886 a round trip from Boston, using both the Cog Railway and the Carriage Road, cost only $17. Although the amazing little Railway probably didn't need the publicity, it got more than its share when President Ulysses S. Grant made the trip in August 1869. President Rutherford B. Hayes was a passenger in 1877.

About 1930, after some fatalities and injuries, the Railway's operators decided to discontinue the exciting but dangerous use of slideboards. Used only by employees, these boards provided a speedy way for workmen to go from the summit to the Base Station at the end of the day or while checking the tracks. About three feet long, made of wood and reinforced with steel, the boards were set over the "rack," or central rail, and slid down like a toboggan. Levers on each side gripped the flange of the cog rail, and by applying pressure the rider could control the speed of his descent. A skilled and daring operator could make the three-and-a-quarter-mile trip in three minutes, and a record was established at two minutes and forty-five seconds.

In 1931, two events had a profound effect on the Railway's future. In July the Boston and Maine Railroad, successor to the Boston, Concord, and Montreal, which had acquired the Cog Railway by stock purchases, discontinued passenger service on the spur from Fabyans, then decided to sell the Cog.

6. *Railroad employee begins descent to the Base Station via slideboard. In the background is the second Summit House.* Courtesy of New Hampshire Profiles.

The B. and M. had its own financial problems and concluded it could no longer operate the little mountain line. Henry N. Teague, a man of great promotional talent but apparently little money, bought the Cog Railway in 1931, mortgaging his new property for the entire selling price of $100,000. He transformed the Railway, which had rarely shown a profit under B. and M. management, into a busy tourist attraction. As a major improvement, he changed the schedule from two trains daily to one every hour. With the old spur line no longer in use, the turnpike, completed in 1869, became the sole route to the Base Station. This modern six-mile road is now a part of the State highway system.

Under Teague's guidance business quickly improved. On one day in August 1936 nineteen round trips carried 659 people to the summit, more than double the former 300-passenger days. When Teague died in 1951, he left his Mt. Washington property, which included land and buildings, to Dartmouth College to repay a large loan granted by the College to repair damage incurred by a devastating hurricane in 1938.

Colonel Arthur S. Teague, who was no relation to Henry Teague but who had been Henry's assistant since 1934, became manager in 1951; and in 1962 he bought the little Railway from Dartmouth College. It is now owned by his widow, Ellen. It was Arthur

Teague and Lawrence Richardson of the Boston and Maine who devised the complicated switching system that allows one train to use a siding when meeting another train. Prior to 1941–42, when switches were installed, there was no method to allow trains to pass each other en route.

Safety considerations have always been a concern of the Cog Railway's management. Before 1967 the Railway had recorded only one passenger fatality in nearly 100 years of service. A man was killed in 1929 when old Peppersass, which had been on exhibit outside of New England, was brought back to the mountain, renovated, and sent up the track again as part of a celebration. Although only a short ride had been planned, it went to within a half mile of the summit, and as it started down, something went wrong and it hopped out of the cog rail. With no braking action left, the little engine slid faster and faster. All passengers but one jumped. Daniel Rossiter, a publicity agent for the Boston and Maine, was killed when Peppersass left the tracks at Jacob's Ladder. Winston Pote, now a nationally known photographer, was seriously injured when he leaped from the engine. The remains of Peppersass were collected and reconstructed; it is on display at the Base Station.

A later accident on September 17, 1967, was the only other serious one in the Railway's history.

It occurred just before dark when the last train of the day left the summit. As the engine and car passed over one of the siding switches, both vehicles were thrown out of the central cog rail. They slid out of control and finally fell off the track. Despite a massive rescue effort hampered by darkness, eight people were killed and many injured. A lengthy review of the accident by the State Public Utilities Commission determined that the switch had been improperly set, perhaps even tampered with by persons unknown.

There is general agreement that the accident was caused by human error rather than mechanical failure of the equipment. All switches are now closely checked before the trains pass over them, and other safety procedures have been instituted. There have been no accidents since 1967, and it seems likely that the Cog Railway will continue to operate safely for another hundred years, giving young and old alike the unique opportunity to ride up a world-famous American mountain in front of a steam engine.

THE ASCENT

The journey to the summit via the Cog Railway begins at the Base Station, often called Marshfield, situated six miles east of Fabyans, off Route 302.

Named in honor of Sylvester Marsh and of Darby Field, the first man to climb the mountain, Marshfield was hewn out of the wilderness by the crews building the Cog Railway, and it has maintained some of the atmosphere of an early depot. When the engine is at the station, puffing smoke and steam and blowing its whistle, with passengers hurrying about, it is easy to imagine similar scenes occurring at a depot during the early days of railroading.

More a collection of buildings than a village, Marshfield comes to life each spring when company employees arrive to ready the equipment for the summer tourist season. The present Marshfield House includes a gift shop, snack bar, restaurant, and kitchen for employees. Here too are the various sheds and buildings used to house the crews and maintain equipment. A water wheel on Franklin Brook turns a generator for electricity and shop power.

The trains are made up of the engine and one car, either a forty-eight-passenger wooden car or a fifty-six-passenger metal car. On the return trip the engine, which pushes the car up and is not attached to it, backs down the mountain ahead of it. Presently the Mount Washington Steam Railway Company operates eight locomotives, including the new Number 10, the Colonel Teague, first used in the fall of 1972 and built by Niles Lacoss, the Company's mas-

ter mechanic. Passengers will note that all the engines and boilers are tilted, to achieve more efficient
operation while traveling the steep grades.

Passenger rates for a round trip are: Adults, $7.50;
Children, $4.00, but under six, no charge.

Trains run only on weekends from Memorial Day to
mid-June, but daily from mid-June to late June.
They leave the Base Station at 11:00 a.m. and 2:15
p.m., with more trips if traffic demands. The same
daily schedule is in effect from the week after
Labor Day until Columbus Day, subject to snow-
storms, gales, and other antics of the weather. From
late June until the week after Labor Day, however,
trains run hourly, with the first ascent at 8:00 a.m.
and the last descent at 6:00 p.m. If the traffic demands and if the equipment is available, two trains
are run at the same time, about 750 feet apart.

The average grade of the three-and-a-quarter-mile
track is 25 percent, with the steepest point, on
Jacob's Ladder, at 37.41 percent. The trains ascend
from the Base Station to the summit, about 3700
feet, in seventy-five minutes. Descent is about five
minutes faster.

The ascent from Marshfield begins at an elevation
of 2569 feet. Here balsam fir and red spruce predominate in a typically northern forest. The track

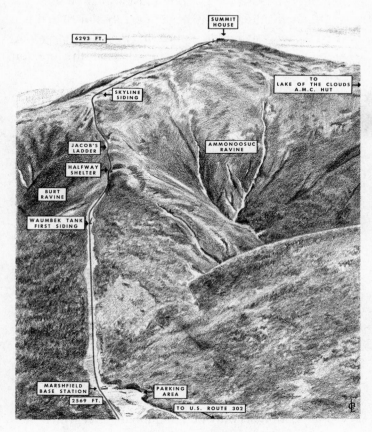

SUMMIT HOUSE

6293 FT.

TO LAKE OF THE CLOUDS A.M.C. HUT

SKYLINE SIDING

JACOB'S LADDER

AMMONOOSUC RAVINE

HALFWAY SHELTER

BURT RAVINE

WAUMBEK TANK FIRST SIDING

MARSHFIELD BASE STATION

2569 FT.

PARKING AREA

TO U.S. ROUTE 302

7. *Artist's sketch of Cog Railway route to the summit. Courtesy of the Mt. Washington Cog Railway Company.*

rises steeply, then levels off until it crosses the Ammonoosuc River, at this point just a small brook. Originally, the Railway began here, but in 1876 the tracks were extended a third of a mile down to meet the regular railroad spur coming in from the junction at Fabyans.

Ahead, around the first of nine curves on the route, can be seen the mile-long grade known as Cold Stream Hill. At this point the train is climbing nearly one foot in three.

Above the hill is Waumbek Siding, and the train stops for water. Both the 8:00 a.m. and the 9:00 a.m. trains continue to the summit without further pause, but other ascending trains pull over onto a siding after the brakeman has set the switch. As soon as the train has cleared the main line, this unique switching device must be reset to permit descending trains to pass. It takes the brakeman about five minutes to make the eighteen moves required to change the switch. When descending, the train must stop above the switch while its engineer and fireman check to see if it has been properly set; then the train continues down the mountain, after which the train on the siding comes out and proceeds to the summit. The ascending brakeman makes all changes in switches for his own and the next descending train, and while the train is climbing, he rides the front platform of the passenger car to watch for obstructions on the track. When descending, the brake-man is stationed at the brake wheels.

From Waumbek Siding the passengers can look back down the broad Ammonoosuc River valley and in particular to the large Mount Washington Hotel. Behind it rises the long Rosebrook Range, the nearer slopes cut with ski trails. North of the valley are Mounts Dartmouth, Deception, and Mitten. South of the tracks are the higher peaks of Monroe, Franklin, and Eisenhower, the latter renamed from Pleasant in 1972 for the late president.

After a few slight curves, the trackman's shanty, also called Halfway House (elevation 3972), is passed. Passengers will note that the trees of this evergreen forest have begun to diminish in size as the elevation increases. To the north is the deep Burt Ravine, named in honor of Henry Burt, who in 1877 founded *Among the Clouds,* the first daily newspaper ever printed on a mountain (see below, page 70). The paths of many landslides scar this ravine and Am-monoosuc Ravine on the south. Both ravines have been cut into the sides of the slopes by streams, and their own sides are much steeper and more jagged than the smoother, glacier-cut Huntington and Tuc-kerman ravines on the opposite side of the mountain.

Here the northwest view expands to include Jefferson Highlands and the Waumbek Hotel complex in Jefferson, and beyond them the long ridge of Mounts Pliny, Waumbek, and Starr King. The fire tower of Cherry Mountain stands out above Mt. Dartmouth, and on the horizon, Mt. Mansfield, highest mountain in Vermont, can be seen 77 miles away on clear days. To the right of Cherry Mountain is Vermont's Jay Peak, 76 miles distant, near the Canadian border.

The surrounding forest, predominantly balsam fir and black spruce, appears as krummholz, growing as low, dense, twisted mats instead of straight trees. At a lower elevation than on the eastern slopes, white birch and mountain ash also appear as krummholz. Trees grow in this pattern because the vertical growth breaks off, especially when frozen, and the tree then brushes out. Since it is unable to grow vertically, it branches horizontally. On this side of the mountain there is no protection from the northwest gales that sweep the snow cover into the ravines and gulleys. Treeline and krummholz therefore begin at lower elevations than on the opposite side of the mountain, where there is more protection from the winds, and the snow cover is deeper.

The treeline is reached at the upper end of Jacob's Ladder (4835 feet), the longest, highest, and steepest trestle on the Cog Railway: 300 feet long and 30 feet above the ground. The name was actually used to

8. *Early photograph of train on Jacob's Ladder. This scene looks much the same way today. Courtesy of* New Hampshire Profiles.

describe the now abandoned trail ascent over the rocky crag to the right, forty years before the Railway was built. From here to the summit, vegetation, thick between rocks and on broad grassy-appearing lawns, is mostly a combination of mosses, rush, heath, and sedges. Everywhere the landscape shows gray, lichen-covered rocks and dark green plants. This is the region of the unique alpine flowers, remnants of the Ice Age thriving above the treeline in a climate similar to that of Labrador, 600 miles north (see below, page 117).

Across the Ammonoosuc Ravine to the south, the beginnings of the Ammonoosuc River can be seen flowing from Lakes of the Clouds. The Appalachian Mountain Club hut of the same name, observed against the skyline, has been a stopping place for hikers since 1915 and holds ninety guests. Behind and to the right of the hut rises Mt. Monroe and the peaks of the Southern Presidentials. It is along this ridge that Ethan Allen Crawford built the first trail to the summit in 1819. Called the Crawford Path, it has been in continuous use since its construction (see above, page 6, and below, page 63).

To the north, Burt Ravine drops away 1000 feet, and above is the ridge joining Mt. Clay to Washington. As the train ascends, the apex of Mt. Adams, second highest peak in New Hampshire, rises above this ridge. Soon, to its left, Mt. Sam Adams, a spur of

Mt. Adams, and then the gentle summit of Mt. Jefferson appear. To the right of the major Adams is the lower summit of Mt. Madison, and beyond is the Androscoggin River valley, bordered on the north and east by the Mahoosuc Range at the Maine border.

After crossing the Westside Trail, the train approaches the Skyline switch and siding. Ascending trains do not pause, but descending trains stop above the switch for inspection by the engineer and fireman. After the switch is crossed, the brakeman leaves his platform and throws the switch. The train backs onto the siding so that ascending trains can pass to the summit. The switch is thrown again, and the descending train moves onto the main track, stops while the brakeman changes the switch once more, then continues down.

Opposite the Skyline switch, northeast of the tracks, the 5552-acre Great Gulf breaks into the magnificent ravine that is now designated as a wilderness area (see above, page 33).

Next on the route up is the Gulf Tank, used only in emergencies. In earlier times the engines made four stops for water, but now the tender holds enough so that only the Waumbek stop is required. Just beyond the tank, the Gulfside Trail is crossed, threading its way to the summit from the northern peaks.

Nearer the summit the Carriage Road parallels the tracks, and the Lizzie Bourne monument (below, page 144) is passed. Then the train makes the short final ascent to the platform in front of the Summit House.

4 The Trails

The trails up Mt. Washington and the surrounding peaks of the Presidential Range offer the hiker almost unlimited variety in both length and difficulty. About a dozen, ranging in length from 3.8 to 15 miles, wind their way to the summit. Some, such as the Huntington Ravine and Great Gulf trails, have extremely steep sections, challenging the most experienced hikers. Others, such as the Davis and Crawford paths, were used as bridle paths and have relatively easy grades.

For the hiker's first ascent of Mt. Washington, two trails are suggested. Both are popular, well worn into the mountain, and marked with cairns (small piles of rock) above treeline, making their location relatively easy to find. Also, each of these trails, at about the half-way point, affords water, shelter from weather, and, should the novice decide that the walk to the summit is too much of an undertaking, a number of interesting sights to see and things to do.

9. *Aerial view of Tuckerman Ravine and the summit. Trails can be seen in the ravine, to its right on Lion Head and in the Alpine Garden, and leading to the summit. Near the bottom of the photograph is Hermit Lake and a warming hut which was destroyed by fire in 1971. Photo by Dick Smith, courtesy of the State of New Hampshire.*

Tuckerman Ravine Trail (4.1 miles to the summit, estimated hiking time 4.5 hours). This trail begins at the Appalachian Mountain Club's Pinkham Notch headquarters on Route 16 and is the shortest trail to the summit from the east side of the mountain. About one quarter of a mile from the start, the trail passes Crystal Cascade, a beautiful waterfall, then ascends gradually as a wide path 2.2 miles to the open overnight shelters at Hermit Lake just below the Ravine. A narrow trail ascends the steep head-wall of the Ravine (see below, page 131) and emerges above timberline at a point known as Tuckerman Junction, 3.6 miles from the base. At this point the trail turns sharply right and, marked by cairns and painted rocks, ascends the cone to the summit, terminating on the Carriage Road just below the top.

Ammonoosuc Ravine Trail (3.86 miles, estimated hiking time 4.5 hours). This trail begins behind the Cog Railway gift shop at Marshfield (one dollar parking fee is charged) and in combination with the upper portion of the Crawford Path is the shortest route to the summit of any trail, east or west. The lower section of the trail passes through woods following the south side of the Ammonoosuc River. At 1.42 miles the trail crosses the river near a pool at the base of some cascades. From this point the ascent is steep, with beautiful views of the Ravine, the surrounding mountains, and the waterfalls, until the trail breaks out above timberline about one hun-

10. *The recently renovated Lakes of the Clouds hut and the summit cone. Photo by Peter Randall.*

dred yards below Lakes of the Clouds hut, 2.46 miles from the base. Here the well-marked Crawford Path is followed 1.4 miles to the summit. Mt. Monroe, just southwest of the lakes, is well worth the short hike to its summit. Many people ride the Cog Railway to the summit and then walk back to the base, using the Crawford Path and the Ammonoosuc Ravine Trail.

Those planning on a Mt. Washington hike are urged to study the Appalachian Mountain Club's *White Mountain Guide* (see below, page 151) before starting their walk. The AMC Mt. Washington map, on sale at the Cog Railway, Carriage Road, and AMC base facilities at Pinkham Notch should be carried by each group of hikers.

For a Mt. Washington hike in summer, each person should bring lunch, a compass, an extra sweater, a windbreaker, and a friend. Sturdy boots are recommended for anyone using the mountain. Trails, even though well marked, are often rough, occasionally wet in places, and not at all suited to those wearing sandals, loafers, or flat leather-soled shoes. High-cut sneakers are acceptable for short walks, but they will not keep feet dry or protect against bruises from the rough rocks that cover the upper portion of the mountain.

For those who may be concerned, first-aid kits are

maintained at the summit, Lakes of the Clouds hut, Tuckerman Ravine, and the AMC Pinkham Notch camp. Usually there is someone at each of these places with first-aid training.

In case of bad or even threatening weather, hikers should immediately retreat below timberline, where the trees can offer protection from the elements. The higher one ascends, the more severe the weather is likely to be, and to turn back is only to use common sense. A number of ill-equipped hikers have died above timberline during the summer in periods of bad weather. Since fog and storms can move into the mountain area in a matter of minutes, the careful hiker will watch for clouds or other signs of a change and will not hesitate to return. Those with a heart problem or who are in any way below par physically should not attempt the climb. Thousands of hikers ascend the mountain in safety every year, however, and for both novice and experienced hiker, the climb is spectacular and immensely satisfying. For the observant and well-equipped hiker the trip should also be a safe one.

Because the fragile plant life on the upper portion of the mountain is particularly susceptible to damage from trampling, hikers are urged to stay on the trails. All are well maintained by the trail crews of the United States Forest Service and the AMC.

Winter climbing on Mt. Washington presents problems challenging even the most expert mountaineers. The severe weather and the necessity for carrying extra equipment makes a trip during this season much more difficult and physically tiring than during the summer. Often parties planning major assaults on the world's highest mountains come to Mt. Washington for training and testing of equipment. No one should attempt to climb this mountain in the winter without proper equipment and only when accompanied by leaders who have ample training and experience in winter mountaineering. Those planning such a winter trip are advised to register with the AMC staff at Pinkham Notch camp. Winter on Mt. Washington generally extends from November through early May. At any time during this period, and occasionally in all other months of the year, snow and severe storms can strike quickly. Even though flowers are blooming in the valley in early spring or late fall, winter conditions may be encountered on the mountain.

Credit should be given the Appalachian Mountain Club and a number of individuals for the fine network of trails that traverse the mountain today. In 1879 the AMC cut the trail to Tuckerman Ravine, and Curtis B. Raymond reopened an older trail, now known as the Raymond Path, from the Carriage Road to Tuckerman Ravine. Two years later, Frank H. Burt and others blazed a route from the Ravine's snow arch to the summit, completing what is now the Tuckerman Ravine Trail.

Ethan Allen Crawford's old Crawford Bridle Path has become one of the more popular hiking trails, winding its way 8.2 miles from opposite the Crawford House on Route 302 to the summit. En route, hikers pass the AMC's Mizpah Spring hut and the recently reconstructed Lakes of the Cloud hut. Both huts, in addition to the others in the AMC Hut System, are open to the public during the summer months, offering overnight accommodations and fine meals. Reservations are required and can be made at the AMC Pinkham Notch camp.

Some of the most important and heavily used trails on the Presidential Range were constructed during the last quarter of the nineteenth century at the personal expense of Prof. J. Rayner Edmands. He hired workers to build the Gulfside Trail (from Madison Huts to Mt. Washington), Randolph Path (which originates at Route 2 and traverses the northern slopes of Mt. Adams to Edmands Col, between Adams and Jefferson), the Israel Ridge Path (which goes to the summit of Mt. Adams from Route 2), Edmands Path (which follows the Mt. Clinton Road to Crawford Path north of Mt. Eisenhower) and the Westside Trail (on the west side of Mt. Washington connecting the Crawford Path and the Gulfside Trail). Although these trails are about 75 years old,

11. Well-worn Crawford Path is visible from the summit toward the cloud-covered Southern Presidentials. Lakes of the Clouds and the AMC hut of the same name are seen at the base of Mt. Monroe. Cloud banks such as this one often move over the mountains, sometimes leaving only the highest summits above the clouds. Photo by Winston Pote.

they are so well made—actually graded paths and paved with flat stones in places—that they show far less damage from erosion and hiker use than many newer trails in the mountains.

The Appalachian Trail, extending 2015 miles from Georgia's Springer Mountain to Mt. Katahdin in Maine, crosses Mt. Washington using portions of the Crawford Path and the Gulfside Trail.

Another of the early trails which is still being used is the Davis Path. The third bridle path to Mt. Washington, it was constructed in 1845 by Nathaniel T. P. Davis, then proprietor of the Mount Crawford House. This trail, which begins on Route 302 south of Crawford Notch near the railroad crossing at Notchland (the site of Abel Crawford's old Mount Crawford House), winds its way along Montalban Ridge to Boott Spur and terminates at Tuckerman Junction, just below the cone of Mt. Washington. Some fifteen miles long, the trail was discontinued because of its length in 1853, but was reopened by the AMC in 1910.

The Boott Spur Trail, on the southern side of Tuckerman Ravine, was built by the AMC in 1900, and six years later the Glen Boulder Trail was opened on a ridge just south of Boott Spur.

Although there is no charge to hikers using any of

these trails, a fee of one dollar per person per night is charged for use of many of the back-country shelters or tent-camping areas. Many of the trails leading to a shelter are marked to show where a hiker can pay his fee and register. Caretakers check these remote camping areas each night.

John Coffin Nazro, a religious fanatic, who believed he owned the mountain and set up toll stations, charged hikers one dollar each. He renamed the mountain Trinity Height and proclaimed the coming of the "Ancient of Days" on July 4, 1851. That day loomed dark and storming, but his predictions were not fulfilled. Nazro, who was opposed in his toll-collecting, gave up his plans and left the mountain. Some years later, however, a man claiming to be John Nazro, U.S.N., presented himself to John H. Spaulding, proprietor of the Tip Top House, saying he wanted to collect back rent. Refused payment, the man left the mountain, never to be heard from again.

5 The Summit Hotels

Since the early 1820's enterprising individuals have sought to offer tourists overnight accommodations on the summit. The first was Ethan Allen Crawford, whose crude, simple, and unsuccessful efforts have already been related. A wooden shelter about twelve feet square was known to exist between 1841 and 1844, but its builder and fate are unknown.

The first Summit House, opened in 1852, was the earliest structure to provide more than temporary shelter on the summit. Horses were used to bring materials over the Glen House Bridle Path, and one of the owners, Lucius Rosebrook, carried the front door up on his back. Built primarily of large rocks gathered at the site, this structure stood on the north side of the summit, well secured against the weather. The building was later enlarged, and remained in use until demolished in 1884.

The original Tip Top House was constructed in 1853, largely because of the success of the first Summit House. It was owned by Samuel F. Spaulding, and among the management personnel was his nephew, John H. Spaulding, author in 1855 of *Historical Relics of the White Mountains,* the first combination history-guidebook on the mountains. The tiny lake in Great Gulf is named for him, and in February 1862, with two companions, the younger Spaulding spent the first recorded overnight stay on the summit in winter.

The Tip Top House was constructed with large rocks for the side walls and a flat roof to be used as an observation deck. About 1861 the roof was changed to permit another story and more room for guests. Its use as a hotel extended until the construction of the second Summit House in 1872-73.

From 1877 to 1884 the Tip Top House served as the office of *Among the Clouds,* one of America's first resort newspapers and the first daily paper ever to be printed on a mountain top. Founded by Henry M. Burt and later operated by his son, Frank, it reported on the daily summer events which occurred on and around the mountain and included articles of both historic and scientific interest. Two editions were printed each day, one early in the morning and another at 1:00 p.m. When the little newspaper reported on the festive coaching parades held each summer at Bethlehem and North Conway, an early edition was carried down the Cog Railway tracks by slideboard before sunup so that readers could have the paper while eating breakfast.

From 1885 to 1908 the paper was printed in its own summit building, offering many people their first opportunity to see an operating newspaper plant. Following the fire of 1908 (see below), it was printed at the Railway's Base Station but was discontinued in 1918 when the Railway closed during World War I. The most complete file of the newspaper is now on microfilm in the Baker Library at Dartmouth College.

In the summer of 1940 the *Mount Washington Daily News* was printed on the summit, a project sponsored by Henry Teague and edited by 25-year-old Richard Carlisle. No other paper has been printed there.

The second Summit House, built in 1872-73 by Walter Aiken, was constructed when the success of the Cog Railway created a demand for larger and more comfortable quarters than those offered by the other two hotels. This building, which could accommodate 150 guests, required 250 trainloads of supplies and cost almost $60,000.

Although the first Summit House and the Tip Top House were really crude affairs, offering only basic accommodations and simple meals, Aiken's hotel

12. *The second Summit House with twelve-passenger mountain wagon designed for use on the Carriage Road. Courtesy of New Hampshire Profiles.*

was as fine as any in the mountains. The large lobby had wall-to-wall carpeting, and guests, who dressed formally for dinner, relaxed to the music of the Mount Washington Symphony Orchestra. The second Summit House remained in use until the fire of June 18, 1908, destroyed it and everything else on the summit except the Tip Top House. The other buildings that were burned included the newspaper office, the abandoned Signal Service weather station, the office of the Carriage Road Company, and the Cog Railway train shed.

Following the fire, the Tip Top House was refurbished and reopened to the public. At the same time there was a proposal to build a huge steel and concrete hotel at the summit, to be serviced by a twenty-mile-long street-car type of railroad. The latter would have replaced the Cog Railway and would have followed a route from the Base Station to Mt. Jefferson, past Mt. Clay, then around Mt. Washington several times, before reaching the top. Lack of money prevented the project from being realized, however, and the third and present Summit House, a more modest structure than the second, was opened to the public on August 22, 1915.

Eight days later fire destroyed the Tip Top House, leaving nothing but its exterior walls. Only the direction of the wind prevented the loss of the newly built Summit House. The Tip Top House was rebuilt soon afterward, however, and was used for a number of years as the Summit House Annex. By 1968 the Summit House had deteriorated to such an extent that its facilities were no longer adequate for overnight guests, and its operation as a hotel ceased, breaking a tradition begun in 1852 when the first Summit House was built.

Another summit building, Camden Cottage, was erected in 1922 by the Cog Railway Company in memory of Patrick Camden, long-time Cog Railway roadmaster. Serving for a while as a shelter for winter climbers, the building fell into disuse following the reoccupation of the summit by winter crews. In later years it was moved from its original location and attached to the Summit House. It was torn down in 1969.

6 The Scientific and Weather Buildings

As already noted, the Indians of New England believed that the Great Spirit lived on the mountain—a superstition that may have been fostered by the fierce storms which swirl about it in all months of the year, and the shroud of mist that frequently covers the summit. Early explorers noted its harsh weather conditions regularly, and it soon became apparent to scientists that the climate of Mt. Washington was far different from the rest of New England, even from the rest of the country. From the first scientific expedition of Belknap and Cutler in 1784 until the present, men have sought to learn more about this small section of New England that closely resembles Labrador.

The first so-called observatory had nothing to do with science. It was merely a framework forty feet high constructed in 1852 by Timothy Estus of Jefferson. For a small fee tourists could ride to the top on an eight-man elevator platform. It was abandoned shortly after construction and was torn down in

1856. Not until the building of the first Summit House, which allowed daily residence at the top, were regular (though limited) weather observations recorded. Temperature readings were taken from June through September at sunrise, noon, and sunset. Records for 1853-54 are included in Spaulding's *Historical Relics of the White Mountains*. Compiled by Nathaniel S. Noyes, a part owner of this first hotel, the records show a high temperature of 66 degrees on June 20 and July 23, 1853, and a low of six degrees on September 16, 1854.

Until 1870 only summer observations had been possible, although many realized the importance of acquiring data during the remaining months of the year. General David Macomber, builder of the Carriage Road, sought to erect a year-round station in 1853 but could not get it funded.

It was left to Charles H. Hitchcock, State Geologist, and his assistant, J. H. Huntington, to provide the impetus for what became one of the great events in the history of the mountain: the first occupation of the summit in winter and the operation of the first mountain weather station anywhere in winter. As early as 1858, Huntington had proposed spending a winter on the mountain, but financial problems and the lack of a suitable building prevented the undertaking until the winter of 1870-71. Huntington and a photographer friend, A. F. Clough, warmed up for the Mt. Washington adventure with a two-month stay in the summit house on Mt. Moosilauke during January and February 1870.

This experience proved the feasibility of the Mt. Washington project, and Huntington and Hitchcock renewed their efforts. Denied the use of the Tip Top House, they were offered the barnlike Cog Railway depot situated at the end of the tracks opposite the Summit House. The financial problems were relieved somewhat when young S. A. Nelson, for whom the crag on Mt. Washington is named, offered to raise money in exchange for being named to the expedition. Finally, the U.S. Signal Service provided enough telegraph wire to extend from the summit to the Base Station, together with other equipment, and the services of operator-observer Sergeant Theodore Smith. Photographers Clough and H. A. Kimball were also part of the team.

During the autumn a room in the depot was equipped with supplies and food, and on November 12 Huntington, for whom the ravine is named, walked to the top and began recording observations the following day. He remained alone until November 30, when the photographers arrived, followed later in December by Nelson, Hitchcock, and Sgt. Smith. Hitchcock, who was in telegraph contact from his office in Hanover, made only a few short visits to the top, but Nelson and Smith remained the entire winter, Huntington most of it, and the photographers for a short time.

Winter climbing on Mt. Washington is common today, though it is best left to the experienced. Prior to 1870 only two parties were known to have made the ascent in winter. During 1870–71, seventy trips were recorded as observatory members went up and down for mail and supplies and many others, including the press, sought out the little weather station. The most difficult ascent was recorded on April 5, when photographer Clough and Charles Cheney faced a furious snowstorm with a temperature of zero and winds of 80 miles per hour.

Although plagued with breaks in their telegraph wire and difficulties in keeping their little room warm, the men passed the winter without major problems, spending their time making observations, keeping records, taking photographs, and performing other duties.

The coldest temperature recorded by these early observers was 59 degrees below zero on February 5, and the highest wind measured was 92 miles per hour on the evening of December 15. They estimated higher winds but dared not venture out to read their instruments. Often the building groaned, rocked, and vibrated for hours at a time during a storm, making sleeping impossible.

13. *The U.S. Government Signal Station, used from 1874 to 1892. Courtesy of* New Hampshire Profiles.

The success of the project convinced the Signal Service that a permanent weather station was not only feasible but desirable, and when these volunteers left the summit in May 1871, Government observers moved in. A new building, known as the Signal Station, was built in 1874.

In January 1877 Signal Service observers recorded the highest wind known to that date, a blast of 186 miles per hour, so strong that it blew down the train depot used during their first four years of occupation. The observers recorded many harrowing experiences during their years on the mountain, but miraculously, no one was killed. These year-round observations continued through the winter of 1886–87 and in summer for another five years, ending in 1892. The Signal Station burned in the fire of 1908 (see above, page 73).

In 1880 the Cog Railway Company built a large observation tower at the highest point on the summit. About twenty-seven feet high and connected to the Summit House by an enclosed walkway, it afforded the mountain visitor an unobstructed view over the summit buildings. It was used a few summers by the United States Coast and Geodetic Survey as a key control point during their first mapping of the region. In 1892 its height was increased several feet, and on it was mounted the largest and most powerful electric searchlight then known. Powered by a dynamo and steam engine, the thirty-six-inch, 200 ampere light was used to learn the effectiveness of signaling over long distances by such means. In those early days the spectacular displays seen nightly for up to 100 miles caused a great deal of excitement. By 1902 the tower was considered unsafe, however, and was torn down.

The present Mt. Washington Observatory began in 1932, largely as a result of the efforts of Robert S. Monahan and Joseph B. Dodge. Monahan, then a recent college graduate and now retired after a number of years with the Forest Service and as Dartmouth College Forester, was the leader of a group that made observations for a few days in the winter of 1926. Dodge, who retired in 1958 after a thirty-six year career as manager of the AMC's hut system, met Monahan on that winter trip, and together they conceived the idea of reoccupying the summit for weather observation and other scientific purposes— particularly radio, which was Dodge's main interest.

By 1932 Dodge and Monahan had worked out the details of the project and were joined by Alexander McKenzie and Salvatore Pagliuca in establishing living quarters and setting up equipment in the Summit Stage Office, which had been offered to them by the Carriage Road Company. Dodge spent most of the winter of 1932–33 down in Pinkham Notch, providing the radio link to the summit and taking his own observations. Data compiled by the station were transmitted via radio to the Blue Hills Observatory in Massachusetts.

The success of that first winter effort, which was carried out as one of many scientific projects in the 1932–33 International Polar Year, convinced everyone that the station should be continued, and after being manned a few more years on a volunteer basis, the Observatory was incorporated as a nonprofit scientific institution in 1936. The following year Henry Teague built the Observatory's present headquarters on the mountain.

One event recorded in the old Stage Office will always be remembered. On April 12, 1934, the crew reported the highest gust of wind ever recorded anywhere, 231 miles per hour. Had it not been for the large chains holding the Observatory building to the summit, it would probably have blown away. In the period of twenty-four hours, the wind averaged 129 miles per hour, and for a one-hour stretch the velocity averaged 173 miles per hour, in each case the highest wind velocities ever recorded for those periods of time.

From a humble beginning the Mount Washington Observatory has become known as one of the best mountain weather stations in the world. It has continued to provide New England with valuable

14. *The present Mt. Washington Observatory, coated with rime. Courtesy of the Observatory.*

weather data while carrying on varied research projects—usually connected with atmosphere physics—for industry, the federal government, and educational institutions. The observers have studied cosmic radiation, the physics of icing, the physical composition of clouds, atmospheric electricity, the cultivation of plants in an artificially maintained environment, and the practicality of the laser as a communications tool. The Observatory has made significant contributions to early studies of the nature of clouds, and it pioneered breakthroughs in shortwave radio in the years before commercial broadcasting began on the summit.

From World War II until the early 1960's, the summit was the scene of a variety of research projects most of which concerned problems of icing on airplanes. Cold-weather clothing and equipment, automobile tires, and even paint have been tested in the harsh winter conditions. Both the Navy and the Air Force have done extensive jet-engine testing at the summit, the latter using several buildings completed in 1956 along the Carriage Road on Home Stretch Flat. The last of these structures was torn down in 1970.

On March 12, 1947, the first airplane landed on the mountain. It was piloted by Carmen Onofrio of Berlin, New Hampshire, who made altogether some forty-two landings in his small plane on the Cow

Pasture, just below the summit. These flights were primarily to bring up supplies for projects under way by Northwest Airlines and the Army Air Force.

Important research in the development of FM broadcasting was conducted by the Yankee Network on the summit beginning in the fall of 1937. Using space rented in the Observatory building, the Network conducted tests during the winter months, transmitting weather reports to the main studios in Boston. The massive FM antenna was completed in 1938. With a decision to operate on a regular basis, the Network began construction of the transmitting station, completing it in 1941. As WMNE Mount Washington, the station broadcast from the summit from December 1941 until 1948, when it closed because of the high expense of summit operation (see below, page 97).

7 The View from the Summit

From the summit it is possible to see at least one hundred miles in all directions over parts of five states and the Province of Quebec. Although the cold, clear days of winter offer the best opportunities for viewing, visitors, on clear days during the summer, can enjoy a panoramic vista extending from the Atlantic Ocean to the high peaks of Vermont. The farthest point visible from the summit is Mt. Marcy, New York's highest peak, 134 miles away.

The following brief description of the view should heighten appreciation of the panoramic drawings attached to the inside back cover of this book.

From the broad platform in front of the Summit House, one overlooks nearly 180 degrees of landscape. At the northeast end the view embraces, from the left, Mounts Clay, Jefferson, Adams, and Madison. Beyond the latter is the city of Berlin, the Androscoggin River valley, and the large Umbagog and Rangeley lakes. Mt. Carmel, just over Adams and

15. Moonlight reflection on icy snow from the summit of Mt.
Washington. In the extreme distance is a reflection on the
Atlantic Ocean, east of Portland, Maine. Nearer is a reflection
on part of Sebago Lake in Maine. Under the moon is Mt.
Doublehead in Jackson, New Hampshire. The bright light at the
right is the main street of North Conway. The reflection in the
center of the picture is on Boott Spur, just beyond Tuckerman
Ravine. Photography by Winston Pote.

recognized by its steep slope, is almost on the Canadian border. The pyramidal Mt. Blue, near Farmington, Maine, is conspicuous in the East. Katahdin, Maine's highest peak, is about 160 miles distant to the northeast but has never been identified from the summit.

From the front of the platform, looking east, the immediate landscape below includes two large ridges projecting from Mt. Washington: Nelson Crag, left, and Boott Spur, right. Pinkham Notch is the valley separating Wildcat Mountain (with ski trails) from Mt. Washington, while the Glen House complex can be seen in a clearing at the base.

Back of the Carter and Wildcat ridges are lesser mountains, and beyond, the broad expanse of the southern half of Maine, dotted with lakes and ponds. Portland, the nearest point on the seacoast, is sixty-five miles away. The large body of water just in front of Portland is Sebago Lake, and nearer still is the long ridge of Pleasant Mountain.

For a better view of the eastern side of the mountain, visitors may follow the stairs down to the parking lot, then walk down the Carriage Road a few yards. Here one can see, below, the Alpine Garden and the upper reaches of two ravines, Huntington, left, and Tuckerman, right.

Pinkham Notch opens to the southeast into the Saco River valley. In this direction can be seen a portion of the towns of Jackson, Intervale, and North Conway, the last lying beside the broad Saco River flood plain and overlooked by Mt. Kearsarge to the left and Moat Mountain to the right.

To the right of Moat is the Sandwich Range, beginning with famous Mt. Chocorua, then Paugus Mountain, the higher peaks of Mt. Passaconaway, Whiteface Mountain, Mt. Tripyramid, and the long ridge of Sandwich Dome. Lake Winnipesaukee, dotted with islands, lies to the right of Paugus. Mt. Monadnock, 102 miles distant, may be visible over the right end of Sandwich Dome.

The best view to the south and southwest is from the outlook just beyond the guy wires of the TV antenna and reached by a short path to the right of the Mt. Washington Observatory. The Crawford Path is clearly seen winding down Bigelow Lawn toward the southern peaks of the Presidential Range: Monroe, Franklin, Eisenhower, Clinton, Jackson (named for Charles T. Jackson, a State Geologist, not for Andrew Jackson), and Webster. About 1½ miles down from the summit are the two Lakes of the Clouds and the AMC hut of the same name.

To the left of the Southern Presidentials is the Dry River valley, extending down to the lower end of

Crawford Notch. Beyond the Notch is the prominent Mt. Carrigain.

To the right of the Southern Presidentials is the Willey-Field-Tom Range, and beyond are North and South Twin Mountains, and the long, jagged Franconia Range (which includes, from left to right, Flume, Liberty, Little Haystack, Lincoln, and Lafayette). To the left of the Franconia Range is Mt. Moosilauke and to its right are the peaks of Killington and Pico, near Rutland, Vermont, ninety miles distant.

A vantage point behind the Tip Top House offers the best views to the west. The Mount Washington Hotel stands out in the wide Ammonoosuc River valley extending from the base of the mountain. The long Rosebrook range forms the western wall of the valley, and to the right are the lower peaks of Deception, Dartmouth, and Mitten. Behind is Cherry Mountain, with a fire tower on its summit. Camel's Hump, seventy-eight miles away in Vermont's Green Mountains, is on the horizon just north of west, and farther to its right on a line with Deception is saddle-shaped Mt. Mansfield, the highest peak in Vermont. Mt. Marcy in New York State, not often visible, is to the left of Camel's Hump, about on a line with the Mount Washington Hotel. Vermont's Jay Peak is just to the left of Mitten. Further to the north are several lesser peaks in Canada, including Mt. Megantic, eighty-six miles distant.

8 The Summit: Present and Future

Most of Mt. Washington is included in the White Mountain National Forest, but approximately fifty-nine acres surrounding the summit now comprise Mt. Washington State Park. In 1867 New Hampshire sold 2000 acres, including the summit, for $500. Dartmouth College, which eventually came into ownership of the summit (see above, page 42), sold its interest to the State in 1964 for $150,000. The sale included the Summit House, Tip Top House, and the Mt. Washington Observatory building, and first option on 9.07 acres of land which Dartmouth had leased to the Yankee Network (now Mount Washington TV) until the year 2010. Both the Carriage Road and Cog Railway companies own rights of way to the summit, and all of these various special interests, including the National Forest, have established over the years, through purchase, easements, and leases, the rights to use at least a portion of the summit.

Since 1971 the State has operated its summit facili-

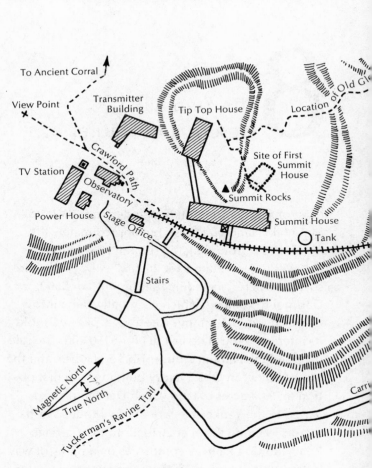

To Ancient Corral

View Point

Transmitter Building

Tip Top House

Location of Old Gle

Crawford Path

Site of First Summit House

TV Station

Observatory

Summit Rocks

Power House

Stage Office

Summit House

Tank

Stairs

Magnetic North

True North

17°

Tuckerman's Ravine Trail

Carri

16. *Plan of the summit buildings.*

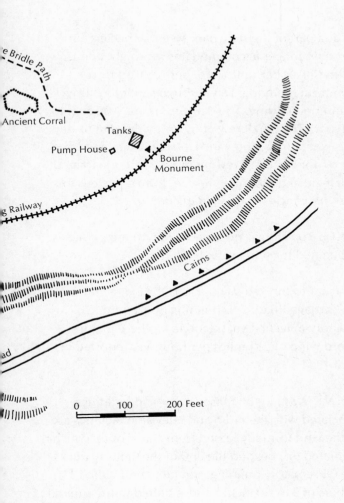

Bridle Path

Ancient Corral

Tanks

Pump House

Bourne
Monument

Railway

Cairns

ad

0   100   200 Feet

ties as a part of the state park system. The Summit House no longer accommodates overnight guests, but its snack bar, gift shop, and restrooms are open from Memorial Day through Columbus Day, weather permitting. The daily hours are 9:00 a.m. to 7:00 p.m. The park crew of five provides day-to-day housekeeping, maintenance, litter pickup, and information for visitors. Crew members, who are trained in first aid and mountain rescue, form a nucleus for any emergencies that might occur.

The Tip Top House, no longer open to the public, is maintained for staff use only.

Adjacent to the Railway tracks is the Stage Office of the Carriage Road. This building housed the Observatory in its first years, and it was here that the record wind of 231 miles per hour was reported in April 1934.

The Mt. Washington Observatory and buildings associated with the radio and television facilities are on the land formerly leased from Dartmouth, which is situated just beyond the end of the Railway tracks. The Observatory building is framed with railroad timbers of 9 by 10 inches and is bolted to the summit rock for protection against the harsh weather conditions. In addition to living quarters for the crew, which varies from two to five depending on projects under way, the little building houses most of the scientific, radio, and telephone equipment, and a darkroom. The crew takes eight weather readings daily, transmitting its findings to the United States Weather Bureau in Portland, Maine. Although the Mt. Washington readings help to fill out the New England weather map, the most important value of the data is climatological: a set of records is being established that can be used for correlations.

In 1972 the Observatory opened the first phase of its museum in a lower floor of the transmitter building, just northwest of the little weather station. By means of dioramas, photographs, natural history displays, and memorabilia, the visitor is afforded a brief introduction to the mountain's man-made and natural history. As a nonprofit institution, the Observatory welcomes new members and donations.

Not open to the public are the facilities of WMTW–TV, owned by Mid New York Enterprises, and WMTQ–FM, owned by Alpine Broadcasting. Studios for both are located in Poland Spring, Maine, although brief weather reports are broadcast directly from the summit nightly over Channel 8.

The television station went on the air in 1954, and its crews and transmitting equipment are housed in the large, flat-roofed TV building in back of the Observatory. The adjacent powerhouse and the large L-shaped transmitter building were originally con-

17. *The summit as it appears today. Only the water tower in back of the Summit House has been removed. At left are the radio and television transmitting facilities. Photo by Dick Smith, courtesy of the Mt. Washington Summit Road Company.*

structed in the late 1930's for use by the Yankee Network FM broadcasting station, which ceased operations in 1948. The present WMTQ–FM radio (formerly WWMT–FM) has been broadcasting since 1958. Immediately in back of the Observatory is the radio tower, and behind it, beside the TV building, is the television antenna. To the left of the power-house is an FM antenna.

In addition to the transmitting facilities, WMTW–TV generates all of the electric power used by the summit facilities and leases space for receiver-transmitter equipment used by many state, federal, and private agencies. Radio transmissions from the New Hampshire Fish and Game Department, the State Police, and trans-Atlantic airplane flights, among others, are relayed through equipment on the summit. ABC network programs are beamed to New England affiliates via the summit, which also serves as a relay point for cable television in northern New England. During the winter, WMTW's large snow vehicle operates between the summit and The Glen, hauling supplies and crew changes for both stations and the Observatory.

Since 1953, four committees or commissions have been appointed by New Hampshire governors to consider the feasibility, acquisition, and operation of a state park on the summit. The result has been the purchase of land and buildings on the summit, the completion of a new sewage treatment system, and, after much study, the presentation of a plan aimed at preserving and developing the physical character of the summit to provide for the public use and enjoyment of the mountain.

The 1973 Mt. Washington Commission, chaired by former Governor Sherman Adams, has proposed the construction of a new two-story building, to be set into the mountain just below the summit. Built of stone and natural wood, it would incorporate the public facilities now offered in the Summit House and would house the Observatory. The Summit House and the Observatory building would be torn down, and the Tip Top House would be restored to its original appearance and used as a museum. The Stage Office of the Carriage Road would also be restored, because of its historic and aesthetic values. The Commission hopes that the facilities of the radio and television stations can be incorporated into the new building or into a new low-profile structure which would be more in keeping with the summit environment.

Although the State no longer feels that overnight accommodations are necessary at the summit, officials believe that the new building should provide shelter from the elements for visitors, a mountain center for search and rescue, and a means for the visitor to learn about an alpine environment unequaled elsewhere in the eastern United States. State legislation is being sought to carry out the project.

9 Weather

The harsh weather conditions found on Mt. Washington have been termed the most severe combination of wind, cold, and icing to be found at any permanently inhabited place on earth. Situated on a major North American storm track, Mt. Washington probably records the worst weather known outside of remote polar regions.

Even in summer, a warm jacket or sweater should be taken to the summit, for the conditions there usually differ greatly from those in the valley. Weather changes rapidly on the mountain, forecasting extreme danger for the unprepared and unobservant hiker. Most of the hiking fatalities have occurred because at the first sign of a change in weather, trampers chose to continue on rather than turn back. For the Carriage Road or Cog Railway traveler, however, the weather conditions often provide unexpected bonuses. An ascent through the fog may find only the summit and other higher peaks poking through the clouds, with a bright sun overhead.

Occasionally, a northwest wind will push the low clouds over the Presidential Range and down into Great Gulf or Tuckerman Ravine like huge waterfalls. Observed under moonlight, the effect is spectacular.

The clearest views are offered immediately after storms are over, and those who have the time to wait will see the mountain in one of its most beautiful periods. Retreating clouds open up surrounding valleys and mountains, creating a spectacle unmatched on cloudless days.

The managers of the Cog Railway and Carriage Road and the staff of the AMC Pinkham Notch hut are in contact with the summit, and weather conditions are posted daily at these base locations.

The single most impressive feature of the weather is the wind, which blows almost continuously, with gusts over 100 miles per hour occurring in every month of the year. The only wind over 200 miles per hour was the record-breaking 231 miles per hour recorded in 1934, but winds over 150 miles per hour are recorded during every month except June, July, and August. The lowest in the high-velocity range for a month is 110 miles per hour for June. The average year-round velocity is 35.3 miles per hour, with January the windiest month, averaging 46. The low month is July, averaging 24.9. The wind exceeds

hurricane force (75 miles per hour) on an average of
104 days per year.

These conditions are created by the Bernoulli effect,
which causes winds gusting along the storm track to
become compressed, and therefore much faster, as
they strike the mountain and flow up over its slopes.
Although all mountains experience this condition,
the effect is greater on Mt. Washington because of
the steepness of the slopes and because of the storm
track, with its continuing winds.

Winds recorded at the summit have shown a marked
decrease in speed over the past thirty years, probably because the construction of many buildings has
raised the level of the fastest wind-flow above the
Observatory's instruments.

Although the mountain's temperatures are far from
the lowest ever recorded, when combined with the
high winds the resulting wind-chill temperature is
difficult to imagine. In severe winter storms it is
possible for exposed flesh to freeze in seconds. The
official record of 47 below zero was in January
1934, and the high for that month is 44 above zero,
recorded in 1950—a variance of 91 degrees. The
record high is 71 degrees, recorded in June, July,
and August during various years, but in June 1945
the temperature dipped to 8 degrees above zero.
The average annual temperature is 27.1 degrees,

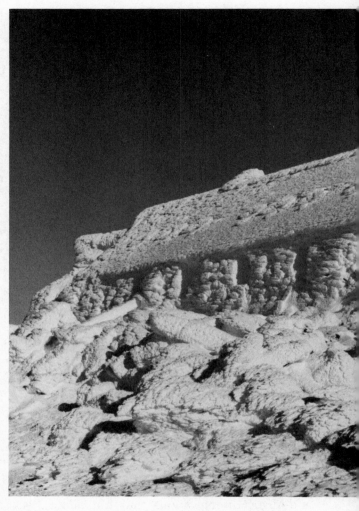

18. *The present Tip Top House, coated with rime. Courtesy of the Mt. Washington Observatory.*

with February the coldest month, averaging 5.6 degrees, and July the warmest, averaging only 49 degrees. The temperature falls below zero about 65 days annually. (see also above, page 78).

Snow has been recorded in every month of the year, but accumulation generally does not begin until November. Snow remains on the higher eastern snowfields until June and as late as September in the depths of Tuckerman Ravine, where skiing may continue till the Fourth of July. Although hundreds of inches of snow may fall on the summit, the cover is rarely very deep, because the snow is blown away by the high winds. There is some drifting in the lee of the buildings.

In contrast to wind velocity, the amount of annual precipitation, especially snow, has been increasing. In February 1969 a record 172.8 inches of snow fell on the summit, with 49.3 inches recorded in a single twenty-four-hour period. The total precipitation (in terms of rainfall) for that month was 25.56 inches. The record precipitation for a single day is 10.38 inches, which occurred in February 1970. Although July normally receives only a trace of snow, too small to measure, a 1957 storm dropped 1.1 inches during a 24-hour period. August has a mean snowfall of only 0.1 inches, but in 1965 a total of 2.5 inches was recorded in a 24-hour period.

Another common weather condition on the mountain is fog, which occurs about 430 hours per month or 60 percent of the time, during portions of about 305 days per year. Because conditions change rapidly, it is common for fog to settle in or dissipate within a few minutes.

Winter fogs cause rime, a deposit of supercooled fog droplets that have frozen on contact and coat the surface of everything on the summit. When the wind is blowing, rime creates the unusual and beautiful frost feathers, delicate banners of rime which build into the wind sometimes several feet in length. The summit is perhaps most beautiful when its buildings and rugged rocks are coated with frost. Wires form great white cables and every blade of grass has its own individual coating, while the exposed walls of buildings are transformed into abstract art forms. Although the tourist might see such a frost display on a small scale, the few men inhabiting the buildings in winter are the ones who experience the most beautiful patterns.

10 Geology

Mt. Washington's geologic history began some 350 million years ago when the sediments that make up the Presidential Range were laid down as layered mud on the bottom of a shallow sea. In time, molten magma from deep in the earth worked its way up through the sedimentary layers, and when it cooled, the rock we know as granite was formed. Coarse pink and finer black and white granite, often exposed in surrounding river valleys, dates from this ancient period. Along the Presidential Range, hundreds of smaller, irregular, sheetlike intrusions remain as white feldspar, white or rose quartz with some flaky mica, and black tourmaline.

The predominant rock on Mt. Washington today is mica schist, formed when compressive forces at work in the earth's crust squeezed, distorted, and folded the layers of mud. The heat generated by the squeezing had the effect of fusing and completely transforming the original layers of mud into the

19. Great Gulf, with Mt. Washington on the horizon at left center. Geologists believe this large ravine was carved by a glacier two and a half miles long. On the horizon at right is the snow-covered Franconia Range. Aerial photograph by Bradford Washburn.

interesting crystalline rock we see covering the summits of the Presidentials today.

Millions of years passed while perhaps as much as a two-mile depth of this folded mass was eroded, at least once, to low hills at nearly sea level. Eventually this area was lifted again, and streams and rivers cut deep valleys to the sea, leaving mountains in their wake.

The remains of those early eroded hills are present today as broad, relatively flat areas surrounding Mt. Washington's summit. Bigelow Lawn, Alpine Garden, adjacent flat-topped spurs, and even the tops of the mountains to the south are remnants of this so-called Presidential Upland, which has been elevated to about 5000 feet.

Into the Presidential Upland are cut Mt. Washington's most spectacular features, the huge cirques or ravines which surround the mountain. These U-shaped valleys, each about a half mile wide and terminating upstream in a large amphitheater, were cut by local mountain glaciers during the Ice Age and predate the last continental ice sheet, which covered New England twenty-five to fifty thousand years ago. These gulfs were created when snow was blown over the sides of the mountains, accumulating to great depths in the sharp stream-cut valleys. Since the climate was colder then, the snow remained year round. Eventually it compacted into glacier ice and with its great erosive power began moving down the mountain grinding out distinctive U-shaped valleys.

The former Tuckerman and Huntington glaciers are thought to have combined below the present Raymond Cataract and probably extended nearly to Pinkham Notch. The former Great Gulf and Jefferson Ravine glaciers formed a river of ice more than two and a half miles long. Other mountain glaciers plucked away chunks of the schist, making the cliffed cirques of Gulf of Slides, Oakes Gulf, Madison Gulf, and, on the northern slopes of the Presidential Range, Bumpus Basin, King Ravine, and Ravine of the Castles.

Other sharper, narrower valleys, less U-shaped in cross section, such as Ammonoosuc and Burt ravines, are thought to have been cut by streams.

The final shaping of the Presidential Range was done by the advance of the huge continental ice sheet, which buried the mountains entirely and rounded out the picturesque notches. Glacial scratches, material deposited by glaciers called glacial till, and erratics (boulders) carried by the glacier and dropped when the ice melted all provide evidence that the ice sheet covered these mountains. The erratics, primarily granite, are found all over the

Range and even near the summit of Mt. Washington but originated in the Ammonoosuc River valley, northwest.

When the great ice sheets retreated, the Presidential Range looked about as it does today from a distance. But the action of the elements had not been completed. The mountains were then subjected to a long period of extreme frost, resulting eventually in the break-up of the mica schist into rough angular blocks, which cover the summits today. These blocks were pushed farther downhill by frost action and formed recognizable patterns now seen as alternate strips of blocks and soil or, when the terrain is flatter, as rock nets, with soil accumulated in the center. This type of action no longer occurs on the same large scale, but small soil cells, perhaps three to ten inches in diameter, are still produced by frost action. The various stripes and nets resulting from the ancient frost are most visible today on Bigelow Lawn and Alpine Garden.

The bulk of the material in this section was taken from the booklet *Geology of the Presidential Range*, by Richard P. Goldthwait, published in 1940 by the New Hampshire Academy of Science as Bulletin Number 1, and now out of print. Material has been used by permission of the author.

11 Flowers and Trees

The plants on the higher elevations of Mt. Washington, unlike those found elsewhere in New England, are in fact closely related to species found hundreds of miles north in arctic regions. It is generally believed that these alpine plants moved south thousands of years ago ahead of the advancing continental ice sheet. As the ice retreated, the plants did likewise, but many species remained on Mt. Washington and on a few other higher elevations in New Hampshire, Vermont, Maine, and New York. The combination of high winds, cold, moisture, and cloudy weather that prevails on Mt. Washington, similar to arctic conditions, proved to be hospitable to the plants; which continue to thrive.

In the alpine zone (4800 to 5200 feet) are found some 110 higher plant species, of which 75 are classified as alpine plants. One, the dwarf cinquefoil, exists in the world only on Franconia Ridge and along the Crawford Path between Lakes of the Clouds and Mt. Monroe. Alpine avens grows only on

20a. *Diapensia is one of the most common alpine flowers. The white blossoms measure about a quarter of an inch in diameter. Photo by Fred Bavendam.*

20b. Lapland Rosebay, one of the most colorful alpine flowers, resembles a miniature rhododendron. These vivid pink flowers are about a half inch in diameter. Photo by Fred Bavendam.

the Presidential and Franconia ranges and in a limited locality in Nova Scotia, while Alpine bluets with white flowers grow chiefly in the White Mountains and on the islands of St. Pierre and Miquelon in the Gulf of St. Lawrence. A species of bluejoint grass was recorded only once, in 1862 near Lakes of the Clouds, and it may never be found again.

Because this alpine area is close to the southern limit for many of these plants, the region has long been a popular spot for botanists, many of whom were among the first scientists to visit these mountains. Their names have been given to prominent natural features: Tuckerman Ravine, Cutler River, Oakes Gulf, Bigelow Lawn, and Boott Spur.

Although the alpine zone is treeless, it is not barren of life. Some form of vegetation grows everywhere —between scattered piles of rocks, in minute cracks in the rock bed, and often in broad lawns that seem smooth enough to mow. These distinctive alpine plants generally appear in communities of several species with the combination of dwarf shrubs— heaths and highland rush being the most common. Widespread bigelow sedge grasses, as well as rush and mountain sandwort, are common near the summit, although this high area is generally poor for botanizing because the plants have been destroyed or trampled by visitors or various construction projects.

The location of many of these species is directly related to snow cover, with certain plants appearing only in areas where snow annually melts at about the same time each spring. The snow assures protection during the winter and provides ample moisture during the spring. Because the growing season is short—only the few weeks between late spring and early fall—the plants are small, but in this period they all manage to complete the cycle from emergence and blossom to fruit. Almost all are perennials, and most store nourishment in their woody bases.

The alpine species are unusual for their small size and often bear relatively large flowers. Photographers would do well to carry closeup lenses if they want to capture on film their full beauty.

Not all of the plants above timberline are alpine; some are subalpine species which manage to exist in the higher harsher altitudes but only in greatly reduced size, primarily because of the strong winds. Below timberline, such species as balsam fir and black spruce grow to commercially marketable sizes, but only a few hundred feet higher, below treeline yet above timberline, they may be only a few feet or even a few inches high. Here they appear as krummholz or dwarf matted plants often growing adjacent to rocks in the lee of prevailing winds. Although some people have considered these smaller gnarled

21. *Presidential Range hikers pass through a section of krumm-holz evergreens. The harsh weather conditions cause these plants to grow as low scrubby bushes, rather than trees. Photo by Peter Randall.*

trees to be centuries old, research indicates that 100 to 150 years is more accurate. The weather on Mt. Washington is so severe that krummholz is likely to be much older in the Rockies, even though the Western treeline is some 6000 feet higher than here.

The best time to see flowers in bloom is from early June to early July. Although some species bloom all summer, most flower early, some while large patches of snow are still on the easterly slopes below the summit. Unless one is hiking from the base of the mountain, the Carriage Road provides the best access to the flower areas, especially the Alpine Garden. Bigelow Lawn, located between the summit and Mt. Monroe on the upper slopes of Oakes Gulf, is also an excellent area for study, but it is reached only by those equipped to hike for several miles over rough, rocky trails. During June, guided flower tours are conducted by the Appalachian Mountain Club, and details can be obtained at its Pinkham Notch camp or at the Boston office. Throughout June and at certain times during the summer, naturalists are in residence at the Lakes of the Clouds hut to answer questions and guide local walks.

One can drive off the Carriage Road at the special parking lots and by walking only short distances observe many species. One mile below the summit, a trail leads south to the Alpine Garden. Those planning to take the well-marked trail, which leads to an excellent area for botanizing, are warned to take along compass, windbreaker, proper footwear, and a friend. (See the section on Mt. Washington climate, above, pages 60–62 and 103–09.)

Those interested in the flowers should remember that none may be picked or touched without specific authorization; and care should be taken to stay on the trails and the rocks. The alpine environment is a fragile one, and man should intrude lightly.

The following are the most common flowers and trees to be observed along the Carriage Road:

Madison Gulf Trail area
(2.5 miles from base).
Northern forest: spruce, balsam fir

Blueberry: low shrub; urn-shaped pink flowers
Bluets: 4 petals, pale blue or white
Bunchberry: 4 large white petals, small, white flowers in the middle
Canada Mayflower or False Lily of the Valley: clusters of small white flowers
Clintonia: 6 petals, yellow
Creeping Snowberry: small evergreen leaves, minute flowers
Goldthread: 5 or 6 petals, white, star-shaped
Hobblebush: shrub; clusters of large and small, white flowers

Interrupted Fern

Labrador Tea: shrub; white flowers, leaves woolly underneath

Mountain Alder: shrub; brownish catkins

Mountain Ash: small tree; clusters of small, white flowers

Mountain Holly: shrub; very small yellowish flowers

Mountain Maple: large shrub; small yellowish flowers in spikes

Painted Trillium: 3 petals, white with pink lines

Red-Berried Elder: shrub; small, white flowers

Red Cherry Tree: white flowers

Rhodora: shrub; flowers showy, purple

Sarsaparilla: very small, greenish flowers in ball-shaped clusters

Shadbush: shrub; showy white flowers, along road below the area

Spinulose Woodfern, Spiney Woodfern

Strawberry: 5 petals, white

White Violet

Willow: shrub; yellowish catkins, male and female on separate plants

The Horn

(4.5 miles from base).

Krummholz forest: low balsam fir and red spruce

Alpine or Bearberry Willow: dwarf shrub, small catkins of two kinds

Bilberry: pink, urn-shaped flowers
Crowberry: needle-shaped leaves, minute flowers
Diapensia: 5 petals, tufted white flowers in clumps
    at side of road all the way up
Heart-Leaved White Birch: bark white or reddish
Highland Rush: grasslike, stiff leaves
Labrador Tea
Mountain Ash
Mountain Cranberry: small shiny leaves
Skunk Currant: greenish flowers, leaves with odor of
    skunk
Three-Toothed Cinquefoil: white flowers, shiny
    leaves

Cow Pasture and Alpine Garden
(7 miles from base).
Easiest flowers to find

Alpine Azalea: 5 petals, small, pink
Alpine or Bearberry Willow: dwarf prostrate willow,
    flowers in catkins
Crowberry: needle-shaped leaves, minute flowers
Diapensia: 5 petals, tufted white flowers
Dwarf Black Spruce: needles whitish
Dwarf Fir Balsam
Dwarf White Birch: brownish catkins
Fir Clubmoss
Lapland Rosebay: showy purple miniature rhodo-
    dendron

Mountain Bulrush or Deer's Hair: grasslike, in
 clumps
Tea-Leaved Willow: larger willow of wet places

This list was prepared by Dr. Frederic L. Steele of the White
Mountain School, Littleton.

12 Animals and Insects

In the woods below timberline, the wildlife is typical of that found throughout the northern forests of New Hampshire. Only by chance or a knowledgeable time-consuming search will one see deer, bobcat, raccoon, porcupine, woodchuck, hare, or any smaller woods dwellers, though many songbirds can be heard.

Hikers in the higher elevations below treeline may happen upon the somewhat rare spruce grouse, and fishermen consider the West Branch of the Peabody River in Great Gulf to be good trout water.

Above treeline the only common mammal is the redbacked mouse, found even among the summit buildings. Several species of shrew and white-footed mouse are less common. An occasional woodchuck may also have a den above the trees.

Slate-colored juncos are the only birds to nest above treeline, but the distinctive voice of the white-throated sparrow is often heard, particularly just below treeline near the mountain huts. The resurgent American raven and various hawks are often seen riding the air currents over the ravines, and many songbirds nest in the woods below treeline.

Some ninety-five insect and spider species have been catalogued in the alpine zone, and sixty-one of these are various species of beetle. Black spiders are abundant, particularly on the various lawns of the Presidential Upland. Many other species seen above treeline are blown up by the strong winds swirling about the mountain.

There are fourteen recorded species of butterfly and moth, and they are abundant on warm sunny days, particularly the brown, medium-sized White Mountain butterfly. It is one of several species dating from the glacial period. The White Mountain fritillary, a small butterfly found only on this range, and the flightless White Mountain locust or grasshopper are among the more unusual insects.

13 The Pinkham Notch Scenic Area

Situated on the east side of the mountain, the 5600-acre Pinkham Notch Scenic Area spreads over the Cutler River drainage, including most of the lower slopes of Mt. Washington from the Carriage Road south to the Gulf of Slides. The Area has two of the most spectacular and best known natural features of the mountain, and one of its most important human resources.

Tuckerman Ravine is famed as the site of the best spring skiing in the East. This large glacial cirque is a catchbasin for snow blowing off the Presidential Range. Next to the Headwall, snows often achieve a depth of seventy-five feet or more, and it is common for patches to remain through August.

The first ski trip into the Ravine was made in 1913 by a trio from the Dartmouth Outing Club, but few others ventured there until the late 1920's. Returning skiers from the 1928 Olympics had both the equipment and the experience to handle the 35 to 55

22. The sharp features of Mt. Washington's eastern slopes are even more pronounced in winter in this view from Wildcat Ski Area. From left to right are Tuckerman Ravine, Raymond Cataract, Huntington Ravine, Chandler Ridge, Great Gulf, then Mt. Adams and Mt. Madison. Photo by Dick Smith, courtesy of the State of New Hampshire.

degree slopes, and they became the forerunners of the now annual spring migration that brings as many as 3000 skiers into the Ravine on a good weekend day during April and early May.

The 2.4-mile trail to the base of the Ravine begins at the AMC Pinkham Notch camp on Route 16. Crystal Cascade, a lovely waterfall, is just four tenths of a mile over the relatively level lower portion of this trail. The ascent to Hermit Lake and its overnight shelters requires about two hours, with the top of the headwall slopes about one hour longer.

There are seven main areas for skiing in the Ravine, of which any or all may be closed because of avalanche danger. Rangers from the White Mountain National Forest are on duty in the Ravine from mid-December until July 1, although the ski season usually begins in late March and extends until the third week of June. In some years, diehard experts ski small patches into July. Early in the season, skiers return to Pinkham Notch via the steep John Sherburne Ski Trail.

Generally, Tuckerman skiing is best left to experts on the steep slopes. Rapidly changing snow conditions can signify danger for the inexperienced skier. Nine people have been killed and many injured during ski season, either from their own falls or from being hit with falling ice. The Mt. Washington Volunteer

Ski Patrol is on duty in the Ravine to assist the Rangers.

Spring skiing is not limited to Tuckerman Ravine. The East snowfields high on the mountain provide challenging slopes, and some experts also ski Gulf of Slides south of Tuckerman.

A beautiful but potentially dangerous feature of Tuckerman Ravine is the Snow Arch. Many small brooks flow over the Headwall to form the Fall of a Thousand Streams, which usually carves an arch out of the huge bank of snow that covers the Headwall. First discovered by Ethan Allen Crawford, the Snow Arch often lasts into August. In July 1854 J. H. Spaulding recorded that the Arch measured 266 feet long, 84 feet wide, and 40 feet high. In recent years it has not achieved those proportions. Because huge chunks may fall from the Arch at any time, it should not be climbed on or under. The first Tuckerman fatality was recorded in 1886 when 15-year-old Sewall E. Faunce was killed by a part of the falling Arch.

Of all the records associated with Tuckerman, the descent of Toni Matt is the most outstanding. In 1931 Charles Proctor and John Carleton became the first to ski over the Headwall from the top. Eventually someone proposed the idea of a race from the summit, down the Ravine and the Sherburne Ski

23. *Thousands of skiiers flock to Tuckerman Ravine in April and May for the most challenging skiing in the East. Photograph by Winston Pote.*

Trail to Pinkham Notch. Called the Inferno, it was first run in 1933. When going down the Ravine, even in a race, skiers made many sharp turns to control the speed of their descent. Matt was an entrant in the 1939 race, held on a day of perfect skiing conditions. He ran directly down from the summit, plunged over the rim of the Headwall, and sped straight to the bottom without the usual turns. He continued past the Hermit Lake shelters and on down the ski trail, leaving some 4000 spectators with one of skiing's great moments. His time was six minutes, 29.4 seconds, and he is the only skiier to have "schussed" the Headwall.

With as many as 14,000 people visiting Tuckerman even during the less popular summer season, overuse has become a serious problem. In all seasons hikers must carry out everything they bring into the Ravine. There are no trash baskets. Wood and charcoal fires are prohibited, but small, portable gas stoves are permitted. No food is sold in the Ravine in any season, and overnight campers must use one of the open shelters located at Hermit Lake. Permits for the shelters are available at the AMC's Pinkham Notch camp.

Huntington Ravine, more rugged and steep than Tuckerman, offers the most challenging rock and ice climbing on the mountain. These pursuits are for experts only, and even they face a serious risk. Many winter climbers have been killed and injured in this Ravine, especially in more recent years when the sport has expanded faster than the skills of some of its participants. Often when one winter climber falls, he pulls his partner along too. Three young men were killed in this manner in January 1969, two in March 1965, and two by an avalanche in April 1964 (see also below, page 143).

The steep, difficult Huntington Ravine Trail is best ascended rather than descended, but it should be avoided in wet weather and by large parties or children's groups.

The recently expanded Appalachian Mountain Club's North Country headquarters in Pinkham Notch is one of the most important human resources connected with Mt. Washington. Founded in 1876 and the oldest club of its kind, the AMC is a leader in seeking protection for the mountains of Massachusetts, Maine, and New Hampshire and in promoting the wise recreational uses of these regions. The Club conducts an increasingly varied program of public service and education, including the maintenance of 350 miles of hiking trails, twenty back-country campsites and shelters, eight huts (see below), and various public education workshops in hiking leadership, group safety, outdoor activities, and the environment. The membership of over 17,000 per-

24. The AMC's Pinkham Notch headquarters at the base of Mt. Washington. Photo by Dick Smith, courtesy of the AMC.

sons is world wide, although centered in New England and New York.

First opened for summer use in 1921, the Pinkham Notch camp has been maintained on a year-round basis since 1926. It is now the center for spring skiing, climbing, and mountain rescue in this area. Overnight accommodations featuring all-you-can-eat family style meals are available throughout the year. The same tasty and bountiful meals are served during the summer in the eight mountain huts which the Club maintains, each about a day's hike apart. The hut system stretches from Carter Notch in the east to Lonesome Lake in Franconia Notch. Among the new buildings at Pinkham Notch is the Joseph B. Dodge Center, named in honor of the man who served as manager of the hut system from 1922 until 1958. Every year more than 30,000 hikers enjoy these facilities, which are staffed and provisioned by young people. Reservations are requested for all accommodations. Details on membership and other Club activities are available at Pinkham Notch camp or at the main headquarters, 5 Joy Street, Boston, Massachusetts 02108.

14 Fatalities

During good weather the ascent of Mt. Washington is a rewarding experience. More than 50,000 hikers reach the top annually without difficulty. But storms of frightening suddenness and intensity can strike the mountain in any month of the year. Also, many people underestimate its size in relation to their own ability. When combined, these factors sometimes result in the deaths of the ill-equipped or stubborn hiker. Those ascending via the Mount Washington Cog Railway and the Mount Washington Carriage Road have little to fear from the weather. Both of these public utilities are closed if conditions are too severe. Hikers, when bad weather threatens, even if they are well up the mountain, should return to treeline where there is protection from the winds and trails can be followed down in the fog.

Frederick Strickland, 29, of England, the first recorded fatality on the mountain, died October 19, 1849, in Ammonoosuc Ravine after losing his way on the Fabyan Bridle Path during an early storm. Since that time, fifteen others are known to have died from June through September as a result of exposure and exhaustion on Mount Washington and adjacent Presidential Range peaks. More than forty others have died as a result of falls, ski accidents, drowning in valley streams, or exhaustion and exposure to physical elements.

The most recent death from exposure occurred on September 12, 1962, when Alfred K. Dickinson, 67, of Melrose, Massachusetts, died at the top of Nelson Crag during bad weather. On July 19, 1958, Paul Zanet, 24, and Judy March, 17, of Dorchester, Massachusetts, died as a result of bad weather on the Crawford Path, only a quarter mile from the summit.

Perhaps the best known fatality occurred in September 1855, when Lizzie G. Bourne of Kennebunk, Maine, died just below the summit at a spot now marked by a monument near the railway tracks. Lizzie, her uncle, and his daughter, began the ascent from The Glen House about 2:00 p.m., planning to spend the night on the summit. By 4:00 p.m. they had followed the Carriage Road as far as it had been built and stopped at the Half-Way House. Workmen urged them not to continue, but they pressed on and were met two miles below the summit by two men going down. To that point, the weather had been clear, but a strong wind began to blow and the party had difficulty in climbing, especially as it became darker. Because Lizzie was showing signs of exhaustion and because they did not know the way to the summit hotels, they lay down to spend the night. Lizzie died sometime before 10:00 p.m., partly as a result of her exhaustion and partly because of a heart defect. The death of the 23-year-old girl, the second fatality to have been recorded on the mountain, made headlines throughout New England.

There have been many near fatalities, and several are reported each summer, although few match the experience of Dr. B. L. Ball during October 25–27, 1855. An extensive traveler and experienced mountaineer, he had planned to climb the mountain with friends, but after delays, he decided to make the ascent alone. In a storm, he made his way to the Half-Way House, where he spent the night. Here workmen told of the recent death of Lizzie Bourne, but he was determined to continue, protected against the drizzle with an umbrella. For most of the day he labored against the high winds, struggling as he broke through the snow crust. When he finally decided to retreat, he had lost the path and was forced to spend the night huddled between two rocks with the umbrella overhead. The next day he attempted to find his way and once saw searchers, but they could not hear his calls. He dragged himself along on frozen feet for hours, finally returning to his former resting place to spend another night. On the third day, searchers looking for his body were surprised to hear calls from the Doctor. He recovered, but it was nearly five months before he regained even moderate use of his hands and feet. With only an umbrella for protection, Dr. Ball had survived sixty hours on the icy mountain without food or drink in a winter storm. He recorded his adventure in a book, *Three Days on the White Mountains,* published in 1856.

A lesser known but perhaps even more impressive feat of survival was accomplished by 58-year-old Max Englehart in 1925. By the Columbus Day weekend, all of the summit buildings were closed with the exception of the Summit Stage Office of the Carriage Road. Englehart was hired as caretaker of the little building and to serve coffee to Carriage Road customers.

From Friday, October 9, until the following Monday, a heavy snowstorm, accompanied by high winds, buffeted the mountain. By Sunday noon, Englehart had used all of his firewood and decided he had better go down, despite the storm. He left a note saying he was leaving for Tuckerman Ravine.

On Monday, climbers from The Glen House reached the summit after a terrific battle with the elements. They found Englehart's note and inquired about him when they reached The Glen House late on Monday afternoon. Joe Dodge, Manager of the AMC's Pinkham Notch hut, and his assistant, Arthur F. Whitehead, were notified and a search began Tuesday morning. Battling another storm, the men made their way to the summit but found no trace of Englehart. On Wednesday, Dodge and Whitehead started on foot from Pinkham Notch to search the Tuckerman Ravine area and about mid-day heard Englehart's cries for help.

After leaving the Stage Office, Englehart had headed for Tuckerman Ravine but was unable to find a way down, so he spent the first night in a hole in the snow at the edge of the Ravine. He wandered around on Monday and was forced to seek shelter for a second night on the cone of the mountain. By Tuesday morning he was so desperate that he just slid down into the ravine, suffering some injuries but surviving the quarter of a mile ride. He found shelter behind some rocks on Tuesday night, and on the following day his cries for help were heard by the rescuers.

With great difficulty, Dodge and Whitehead carried Englehart down to Pinkham Notch, arriving after dark. Although he lost part of one heel and all of his toes because of frostbite, Englehart, like Dr. Ball, survived three days in a winter storm on Mount Washington, records of accomplishment no one hopes to match.

The list of fatalities is much shorter than it might have been only because of the sacrifices made regularly on behalf of hikers by employees of the New Hampshire Fish and Game Department, Forest Service Rangers, members of the Observatory crew, employees and members of the Appalachian Mountain Club, the Ski Patrol, and other volunteers. On numerous occasions these men have faced below-zero temperatures and high winds to search for lost climbers or to carry down those who have been injured. Often searchers hunting for one lost group will come across others who have experienced trouble because of the weather or falls. During the winter, climbers are asked to register at the AMC Pinkham Notch camp before each trip, and to check out upon returning. Too often, search crews have set out when the object of the search was already home.

Further Reading

In his excellent *Bibliography of the White Mountains,* Allen H. Bent says that these mountains "have had more written about them, probably, than any other mountains, the Alps alone excepted." His book, published in 1911 by the Appalachian Mountain Club and reprinted in 1971 by the New Hampshire Publishing Company, Somersworth, New Hampshire 03878, 97 pages, includes numerous histories, many guidebooks, and hundreds of magazine and newspaper articles. Since 1911 the list has expanded considerably, but this is the basic volume for the collector of White Mountains printed material.

It is unfortunate that most of the best books are out of print and available only at high prices from rare-book dealers. In offering the following reading list, we are limiting it primarily to the most important books currently available from publishers or in North Country bookstores, gift shops, and outdoor equipment stores.

The Story of Mount Washington, by F. Allen Burt, University Press of New England, Hanover, New Hampshire 03755 (1960), 315 pages, illustrated. The most complete history of the mountain, it is the only book to offer detailed information on events occurring since 1916.

Lucy Crawford's *History of the White Mountains,* originally published in 1845 and most recently reprinted in 1966, University Press of New England, 305 pages, illustrated. Lucy was the wife of Ethan Allen Crawford, and her book tells the history of the family and the early development of the Crawford Notch area. The new edition is edited by Stearns Morse.

Scenery of the White Mountains, by William Oakes, with 16 plates from drawings by Isaac Sprague, originally published in 1848 and reprinted in 1970 by the New Hampshire Publishing Company, 43 pages folio size. Oakes was a botanist, but his book covers many points of interest in addition to the beautiful scenic lithographs. The reprint has an introduction and excellent commentary by Sherman Adams, former Governor of New Hampshire and a long-time resident of the mountain region.

Railway to the Moon, by Glen M. Kidder, published by the author, Davis Substation, Acton, Massachusetts 01720 (1969), 184 pages. A comprehensive pictorial history of the Mt. Washington Cog Railway, including considerable information on the Company's engines and passenger cars. More than 200 photographs.

The A.M.C. White Mountain Guide, published by the Appalachian Mountain Club, 5 Joy Street, Boston, Massachusetts 02108, 20th edition (1972), 576 pages with seven removable maps. A must for hikers, this book gives complete descriptions of all trails in New Hampshire, including the length of each trail and the estimated hiking time. The AMC also publishes *Appalachia,* a semi-annual journal devoted to topics ranging from mountaineering and canoeing to conservation and history.

Mountain Flowers of New England, published by the Appalachian Mountain Club (1964), 153 pages with 149 color illustrations and 61 figures. For those with a serious interest in the plants of the mountains, this is the most valuable handbook available.

Alpine Zone of the Presidential Range, by L. C. Bliss, published by the author (1963), 68 pages. Excellent coverage of the geology, climate, and flora and fauna of the Presidential Range.

History of New Hampshire, Volume III, by Jeremy Belknap, originally published in 1792 and most recently reprinted by Peter E. Randall, 36 Mace Road,

Hampton, New Hampshire 03842 (1973), 320 pages with map. Depicts Belknap's early scientific expedition to Mt. Washington and contains a geographical description. The new reprint is edited by G. T. Lord and includes footnotes and index.

The Observatory, Cog Railway, and Carriage Road have all prepared booklets relating to their interests.

Free brochures covering many aspects of the mountains, including Tuckerman Ravine, Alpine Garden, and Great Gulf, have been prepared by the White Mountain National Forest. Copies are available at the Ranger stations in Conway and Gorham, Pinkham Notch camp, and many gift shops, or by writing to the White Mountain National Forest, Laconia, New Hampshire 03246.

Of the many out-of-print books, the best and most inclusive is *Chronicles of the White Mountains,* by Frederick W. Kilbourne, published by Houghton Mifflin in 1916. It covers the history of the entire mountains. May be found by checking with New England rare book dealers and in libraries. Other important out-of-print books include the following:

Historical Relics of the White Mountains, also a Concise White Mountain Guide, by John H. Spaulding, 96 pages, Boston (1855 and later editions).

Incidents in White Mountain History, by Benjamin G. Willey, 321 pages, Boston (1856). Later editions are entitled *History of the White Mountains.* Contains the best report of the Willey slide disaster in Crawford Notch, which occurred in 1826.

The White Hills; Their Legends, Landscape, and Poetry, by Thomas Starr King, 403 pages, Boston (1860, with many later editions). This book had an important role in popularizing the mountains during the late 1800's.

Mt. Washington in Winter or The Experiences of a Scientific Expedition upon the Highest Mountain in New England, 1870–71, by C. H. Hitchcock, J. H. Huntington, and others, 363 pages, Boston (1871). The story of the first winter spent on the summit and of the first winter weather observatory.

Mount Washington Reoccupied, by Robert S. Monahan, 270 pages, Brattleboro, Vermont (1933). The story of the beginning of the present Mt. Washington Observatory.

Alpine Zone of Mt. Washington, by Ernst Antevs, 118 pages, Auburn, Maine (1932). One of the best general scientific works on the mountain.

The White Mountains, A Handbook for Travellers, by M. F. Sweetser, Boston, (1876, and many later editions under varied titles). Also known as Osgood's or Ticknor's *White Mountain Guide,* this was in its time the best and most comprehensive of the many guidebooks written about this area.

Index

Winter Cutoff road, 30
Woodfern. *See* Spinulose woodfern
Woodchuck, 129

Yankee Network, 85, 100. *See also* Mount Washington TV
Yellow birch, 28

Zanet, Paul, 144